P9-DFE-943

Down to Earth

But

Looking Up

stories to lift the spirit

Down to Earth
But
Looking Up

stories to lift the spirit

ANDREW J. COSTELLO

ThomasMore®
– An RCL Company –
Allen, Texas

ACKNOWLEDGMENTS
Cover design by Melody Loggins of Zia Designs
Inside book design by Kim Layton

Copyright © 1999 Andrew J. Costello

All rights reserved. No part of this book shall be reproduced or transmitted in any form or by any means, electronic or mechanical, including photocopying, recording, or by any information or retrieval system, without written permission from Thomas More.

Send all inquiries to:
Thomas More
An RCL Company
200 East Bethany Drive
Allen, Texas 75002-3804

BOOKSTORES:
    Call Bookworld Companies 888-444-2524 or fax 941-753-9396
PARISHES AND SCHOOLS:
    Thomas More Publishing 800-822-6701 or fax 800-688-8356
INTERNATIONAL:
    Fax Thomas More Publishing 972-264-3719

Visit our website at **www.rclweb.com**

Printed in the United States of America

Library of Congress Catalog Card Number: 99-74133

ISBN 0-88347-429-8

1 2 3 4 5   03 02 01 00 99

Table of Contents

To my two sisters,

Mary and

Peggy (Sister St. Monica, IHM)

as well as to Mary Cicale

who made many very helpful suggestions

and to Debra Hampton for great editing,

support and improvements for this book.

An Invitation

This book is an invitation to stop and listen to what's happening on Earth.

I often sit here in the cool of the evening trying to understand life's *why* questions. I why? Why am I here in this time, this place, with these people? Why did I make the choices I've made so far? So many it seems were done without enough thought. Why have I been given so many blessings?

This book is also an invitation to look at answers to questions. We all have answers—some that we're sure of, some that we're not so sure of. Questions. Answers. Wonderings. We're always talking to ourselves about something. What have I figured out so far? What do I need to wonder about a lot more?

This book is an invitation to be Earth-wise, to take it all in. It's an invitation to look at all that surrounds us, all that is around us, to:

> ~ see,

> ~ feel,

> ~ hear.

It's an invitation to grasp the way the Earth feels, maybe even the way God feels it all.

Down to Earth But Looking Up is a series of stories and reflections about the Earth and the people on it. It will be a series of images, scenes and themes.

This book is like an old shoe box in the closet or under the bed, filled with old letters, photos, postcards and match books—bringing back memories, stories, connections with people we've met, loved, forgotten, places we've been to and questions about our decisions and where they have taken us so far.

This book offers the hope that we'll see the persons, places and things on our Earth, in our garden, in our desert, in a new way. The hope is that we'll see all that is around us on Earth as gift. The hope is that we'll take better care of everyone and everything on this wonderful planet we call home.

The Earth listens. The Earth feels. The Earth cries. The Earth knows. The Earth remembers. The Earth forgives—sometimes. Too often I, formed of Earth, don't remember, don't forgive, or I feel I can't forgive. Too often I don't listen.

This book can be opened up and listened to at any point—like life—so long as we listen with compassion, with forgiveness and with love.

Genesis

'Every story has to begin somewhere and when the story begins, especially when it's our story, we listen.

Once upon a time we began . . .

Listen to the story—the story of the Earth. It's our story.

The Earth is filled with life. The Earth breathes. It's breathing in and breathing out. Feel its breath. Feel the wind. Take its pulse. Catch its spirit. Walk in the garden in the cool of the evening.

Walk with God—the God of Creation, the God of the Garden. Talk. Listen. Love. Give thanks.

Take off your shoes. Feel the Earth under your feet. It's God's creation, God's gift. All is gift. All ground is holy ground.

Listen to the basic choices God gives us.

Listen to the basic warnings God gives us.

The tree of the knowledge of good and evil is in the Garden.

The tree of life is also in there.

God also gives us helpmates.

Talk. Communicate. Help one another. Make good choices.

Choose well.

Beware of snakes in the grass.

See the sparrows and the blackbirds. Watch the monkeys in the trees. Watch the willows wave in the wind. Watch the leaves fall in Autumn. Watch the snow in Winter. Watch for new life rising in Spring and flourishing in Summer.

Stand tall as rising wheat. Find time to look at the heavens. See the light. Stop to see the sun rise and the sun set. See the moon, the stars and the dark—the vast vault of sky.

And all is good.

Stand still on the shores of Earth's lakes and rivers, its seas and oceans. Water, water, everywhere . . . Notice that the waters are like life: sometimes shallow, sometimes deep, very deep.

Come to the waters.

Walk into the water. Be careful in the shallow places. Life is everywhere— if only we will see it. Go further. Dive deep into its depths. Be baptized in the waters of life. Know that we're swimming in the ocean of God.

And all is good.

The Earth is interesting. Firm Earth, fluid waters . . .

Life. Death. Time. My time. Am I having "the time of my life?"

Take time to read the story.

Listen. Just listen. Listen to what is happening on the Earth.

See this. See that.

And all is good.

Listen . . .

The Sounds
of the Fall

The Earth Listens . . .

Too often we don't.

Too often we are too busy, too cold, too narrow in our concerns. The result: we don't laugh, cry, or feel enough. We find ourselves *out of touch*.

Prophets see. They listen. They know. They're *in touch*. They speak.

"Hear the word of the Lord . . . "

See the word of the Lord.

Isaiah, the prophet, told us we have eyes that don't see, ears that don't hear, hands that don't help, minds and hearts that are closed, when they ought to be open.

Down deep, don't we really know God wants to walk with us, talk with us, and be our God? Come on. Be honest. We know life is a play we write with God. Sometimes it's comedy; sometimes tragedy; but it's always drama. We know that Earth is the stage, as Shakespeare put it, and even though there's a cast of millions, at times each of us has a leading role.

Let's be honest. We know this.

Too often we don't want to cooperate or co-author or be on stage with God. Talk about being a self-centered actor.

We hide in the tall grass, behind trees, behind words, behind excuses like, "I don't believe all this." And whenever we hear God's footsteps in the Garden in the cool of the evening, we hide.

We sin. We fear. We become numb. We become dumb.

Sometimes we want to sink deep into the Earth from which we came. We use our creativity to find more and more creative ways to escape. We forget we are made in the image and imagination of God.

And when this happens, all is not good.

When we're not dancing the eternal dance with God, we can miss half the laughter of life.

We can miss much of life's music, especially the divine symphony, when we don't stop to listen.

The earth is playing. Listen.

Close your eyes. Hear the roaring ocean and the shifting tides within us, without us.

Pick up a conch shell. Listen carefully to the sounds of the sea within.

Listen to the breath and wind of the Spirit moving wherever it wills—across the waters, through the Garden, and through the trees.

Watching swaying, shifting trees in a breeze, violinists playing, an orchestra.

We can be blind. We need to open our eyes and see a hawk high in the tree. See the arms of the oak tree reaching for the sky. Watch the rivers as they rush or take their time—rolling down toward the sea.

See that all is good.

See people.

See the children. See the elderly. See their skin: the young, supple skin of the kids—like new leaves of Spring—and the wrinkled skin on the faces of the elders—like the red, orange, tan leaves of Autumn—splashes of color before the Fall.

Listen to the Earth!

We sin.

We know this. We remember when we heard the whisper, "Take and eat." And we bit into sin.

The Earth knows. Beware. It knows when trees are destroyed and when soil is ruined.

The Earth hears the cries of the poor and the moving in of the bulldozers of the rich.

The Earth remembers. She remembers how and when all the good started. The Earth feels God's fingers forming and sculpting us from the clay of Earth—our Mother's womb.

The Earth feels God's knees, as God kneels down, needing us, kneading Earth like bread, forming our body like bread rising, God breathing life into us—like a parent leaning over a crib, whispering in awe, "This is my body." "This is my blood."

"It's a girl!"

"It's a boy!"

"It's me!"

"Adam!" "Eve?" "Where are you?"

"Here I am, Lord, often hiding, because I'm often afraid."

And fear can crush the creative spirit in and out of us.

I forget that like everyone else I am a breath of fresh air—created by the Holy Breath of God—the Giver of Life.

"Come Holy Spirit!"

I often forget and fall, down to Earth, half dead, lying here in a field of dry bones!

"Come, Holy Spirit! Rush upon all of us with a breath of fresh air!"

Resurrection and new life is the eternal call.

The Earth rejoices when I listen to that call, when I awaken, when I come back to life, when I decide to come forth. The tomb opens, Mother Earth's womb opens again, and I come forth breathing new life again and again.

Again and again I forget. And then I remember.

Life and then death and then life again. That's the drama. That's the plot.

And when I die the Earth weeps. The Earth cries when the breath of life leaves me for the last time. The Earth feels it when I am lowered into the grave—into the dust from which I came.

And our children stand there crying over our grave, "This is my body which was given to me. This is my blood which was poured out for me."

Listen . . .

My First Bicycle

'Every kid has to have their own bicycle. Right? Well, I didn't.

In the early 1950s, in Brooklyn, N.Y., twelve was the minimum age for becoming a paper-boy. Many of the kids delivering the *Brooklyn Eagle* arrived at the newspaper office on bikes. I didn't. I envied them, these "big wheels," watching them getting off their bikes, as if they were getting off a horse or a motorcycle.

I arrived at work those first few weeks on foot.

I wanted a bike, and wants become needs.

I needed a bike, so I began saving money and began my search for a second-hand bike.

There it was—on Third Avenue—under the highway in the local bicycle store: basic bike—and it cost only one twenty dollar bill—an Andrew Jackson.

It was me. Adolescent. Thin. It was probably 12 years old too.

I bought it—a second-hand bike—sheer simplicity. It was merely a frame with thin black tires, black seat, black pedals. It was mine—easy to bring in and out of the cellar—easy to ride.

But no boy lets anything stay "as is." Everything needs to be personalized—improved—decorated—made one's own.

The frame looked like it had acne. It was pockmarked, so I sanded off a layer and a half of blue and red paint. Then I painted it total red. I saved more money and bought my bike brand-new silver fenders—with a red reflector for the back.

It wasn't an English bike with those neat brakes on the handles or a switch for different speeds. I don't even remember whether bikes like that were around our neighborhood at the time. It was an American bike—the brakes were applied by reversing and jamming the pedals. The speed depended on hills and how fast one could pedal.

I discovered wheels. I discovered speed. I discovered freedom. Like the Wright Brothers I began to fly. They started with bicycles. Why couldn't I?

It was my first chance to roam the earth.

It was the early '50s and there weren't many cars roaming our streets. So it was safe to ride the hill from our house on 62nd Street and Third Avenue to the Narrows, down to the New York Harbor at the 69th Street pier, to watch the fishermen and the Staten Island Ferry, and the ships heading for and leaving Manhattan and New Jersey, and to see the Statue of Liberty in the distance.

Time flies. The new becomes old. We get used to what we own. And sometimes even a kid has to make some basic choices.

Decisions. Decisions. Decisions.

It's good for a boy to have to buy his own bike and to learn how to make decisions.

The decision I had to make was this: Should I buy a basket for the front of my bike, or should I keep on riding with my newspaper bag over my shoulders? The basket would certainly make work much easier. However, the wire basket in front would change the appearance of my bike from being a symbol of freedom to simply being a paper-boy's bike. Yes or no? Work or pleasure? Status symbol or means of delivery?

I chose the basket.

Now, looking back, come to think of it, I don't remember anyone in my family ever saying anything concerning my bike and the various decisions I had to make about it.

Good. A kid growing up needs things like that to happen, to make his or her own decisions, and to keep rolling on and on around the world and across the Earth.

Down to Earth
But Looking Up

Though I am "down-to-earth," I find myself pulled upward toward more.

I find myself looking up into the sky, to mountains, to tall buildings, to stately trees, steeples, to the Cross, to stars in the night.

And as I grow older and wiser I find there's more than meets the eye. I find myself stopping to watch a bird soar and swim in the wind. Work can wait. Wonder can't. More and more praising God for all this beauty. Thank you, God. Thank you for surrounding me with all this goodness. I'm just beginning to recognize these gifts of earth you have given me. And there's more.

Much more.

People! People mean words, music, jokes, card games, projects, planting and harvesting, manufacturing and shipping, buying and selling, meetings, coffee breaks, weekends, vacations, sports, hospitality, cocoa and chocolate chip cookies in Winter, potato chips and pop in Summer, comments during chance meetings inside shopping centers and outside churches.

Yes, Lord here I am working at my desk or on the road. I am one with the sweat and the body strain of making a living. Yet, Lord, more and more, I find myself longing for your Spirit in the everyday and in everyone. People may look at me and wonder, "What's the matter?" as I search for you in the matter. "You are," as someone said, "the beyond in my midst."

More or less?

I've chosen *less* too many times; now I'm yearning for *more*.

My spirit wants to soar, needs to soar, was a caged, dull, tamed bird that had forgotten how to sing—how to fly.

No wonder the Spirit is pictured as a bird—flying above all, flying through the air, free, flying over garbage dumps and million dollar shopping malls.

More. A higher life.

No wonder the Biblical songwriter wrote, "I glance up to the mountains. Where is help going to come from?" (Psalm 121)

Everyone needs help. Everyone deserves it. Everyone longs for more space. Everyone deserves Sabbath. Everyone needs a fig tree to sit under in the cool of the evening, where we can contemplate the moon and the stars, people and places, and so much more.

Stop signs. The wrong stop signs have stopped me.

The right stop signs are in my house, in my family, in my work, in recreation. I won't see you in these places unless I stop, unless I reach out for peace, and for moments of grace.

I'm beginning to understand why people go fishing. I'm seeing the importance of gardening or knitting or making bread or reading or praying or going to church, mosque or synagogue. It's in these moments that I begin to be more in touch with the More. And in these moments I recall the days when I reached for Less—eating, drinking, sleeping, working or running too much—unhealthy escapes to take the edge off feelings of being less.

More or less?

We long for rest, yearn for peace, thirst for places and times to sit with a book, to rest, think, pray, to be in silence.

Lord, I am waiting for your grace. I am aching for More. Here I am Lord, never satisfied.

Lord, fill me, with you.

Thank You.

The Cookie Jar

'Everybody knows you don't open your Christmas gifts up before Christmas.

Not a seven-year-old kid named "Timmy". He just stood there waiting for the priest to open the Christmas gift he had just handed him.

The priest didn't know. He simply took the gift from Timmy, said, "Thank you," and turned to someone else.

He wasn't being rude. There was a small crowd standing there. Timmy and his parents were only a few of about fifteen people standing in the vestibule of the church after Mass that last Sunday before Christmas.

Timmy had seen the big cookie jar while Christmas shopping with his mom. Pointing upward at the jar, he said, "There's Father Frank. He's on sale."

His mom said, "Where?" Timmy kept pointing and smiling at the cookie jar. "Come to think of it," his mom thought to herself, "it *does* look like Father Frank."

It was one of those large cookie jars, a shiny clay monk dressed in a brown robe, wearing a big, beautiful smile.

Father Frank wasn't a monk. But Father Frank was big and tall, had a great smile and a great stomach. Everyone loved him and he loved everyone. And he loved cookies too.

Timmy knew this. He had seen this every time Father Frank came over to the school—always arriving at lunch time—always reaching for cookies.

So when he saw the cookie jar in the store, Timmy wanted it. He wanted it as a Christmas present for Father Frank.

Timmy handed his gift to Father Frank who said, "Thank you" and placed it on a table there in the church vestibule. That was it. He didn't open it on the spot. Timmy waited. Several people wanted to say things to Father Frank—especially about a story he had told in his sermon.

Timmy kept waiting. He waited with a devil of a smile on his face. He wanted to see Father Frank's face when he opened up the box and saw the cookie jar.

His parents waited with him. They understood Timmy. They knew he had looked forward to this moment all week.

Finally, when everybody had finished their business, Father Frank noticed Timmy still standing there. He saw Timmy's smile. He saw Timmy's parents and asked, "Can I help you?"

They said nothing. They waited for Timmy to speak. He smiled a big smile and said, "Aren't you going to open your Christmas present?"

"Oh," and then he almost said, "What Christmas present?" Father Frank was taken back a bit. He needed a second to figure out what Timmy meant. At last he turned, picked up the box, shook it saying, "You mean this?" He finally remembered the box Timmy had given him.

"Yes!"

The moment had arrived. He read the tag taped to the wrappings, "To Father Frank, Merry Christmas, Love, Timmy." He said, "Very nice" as he quickly unwrapped the gift. He opened the box. Pause. A moment of silence. Then came Father Frank's famous smile, "Ho, ho, ho. Wonderful, Timmy! Very nice. Thank you."

"You're welcome Father. And it's full of cookies! Aren't you going to have one?"

Father Frank opened up the top half of the monk and took out a big chocolate chip cookie and offered cookies to Timmy and his parents from deep in the monk's belly.

What a smile. What a moment. What a gift.

Father Richard Frank told me this story a short time later. He caught me smiling at his cookie jar in the kitchen of St. Mary's rectory, Honesdale, Pennsylvania.

Six months later, June 28th, Father Richard Frank died.

What ever happened to that cookie jar?

And where is Timmy now?

Earth's Firsts

The first time a mother sees the wet, slippery, rubbery body of her new-born baby . . .

The first time a father holds his new-born baby and he fits and cradles perfectly in his hands and arms . . .

The first time a kid sees her shadow on a long cement sidewalk and turns around to see if the shadow is on the other side and it isn't and she tries to figure it out . . .

The first time a small child hears crickets in the park and stops to see where the sound is coming from and discovers a symphony of sound, stereophonic music, from every blade of grass . . .

The first time a child sees the ocean, sees waves crashing in on the beach, waves rolling in one after the other, sea gulls fishing, singing, screaming, rejoicing in creation . . .

The first time someone teaches a kid to put a conch shell up to her ear and she does and she discovers the wonder of the ocean in a shell . . .

The first time someone sees a field of woolly sheep dressed in gray white Irish sweaters munching on sweet grass on a green hillside . . .

The first time a person falls in love and finds there is nobody around to talk to about these wonderful feelings, because they don't even know what feelings really are yet . . .

The first time a kid gets her own yo-yo and makes it "walk" on the school yard macadam in front of her friends . . .

The first time a little girl sitting in the back of a family van sees a rainbow after the rain and shouts to everyone to look out the window, and the car is filled with "Wows!" and her father is able to pull the van off to a rest area so all can get out to see the rainbow as a family, not just out a window, but outside on the big screen of the western sky . . .

The first time a boy discovers that you can make rocks skip along a lake by simply finding flat rocks and throwing them low and sidearm and close to the water . . .

The first time a child sees fireworks on the Fourth of July together with a couple of thousand people "oohing" and "aahing" at each new burst and splash and crash of lights and sparks in the dark summer sky . . .

The first time a boy has his own water gun, and he and his father have a great fight—in front of their house after supper—his father with a small light green plastic water pistol—the boy with a Superblaster both of which his father had bought that afternoon on the way home from work and his mother is laughing as she is looking out the front window watching her husband and her son having a great time . . .

The first time kids go to an art museum on a class trip and discover big people's drawings, paintings and sculptures—and one little girl has a dream . . .

The first time a kid goes on a roller coaster ride and his parents won't go on it with him, "It's too scary for us!" and he sees them down below at the fence looking and waving as he goes flying by and after the ride he heads back to his parents standing tall, feeling like a grown-up . . .

The first time a couple is making love and it's on their wedding night and they're laughing not just because they waited, but because several of their friends joked that they hadn't . . .

The first time a person goes hiking in the mountains and after a long climb up, way up beyond the tree line, reaches the peak of a mountain and all is clear for miles around . . .

The first time a retired airline pilot has the time to plant tomatoes after hearing from all his friends about their tomatoes and cucumbers and zucchini, and it's September and everything is coming up tomatoes—big, red, beautiful, juicy tomatoes . . .

The first time a person goes on an airplane and everyone seems so relaxed and it seems that no one has a clue to how nervous I am right now . . .

The first time a person experiences the presence of God: seeing a baby's fingers or a red rose or a splashing rust-orange sunset or a waterfall . . .

The first time a person makes a double layer cake with icing or a loaf of bread or Jell-O . . .

The first time a kid reads in public, at school or at church, and she is nervous and her Mom and Dad are nervous, sitting down there, front row and center, holding hands and crying tears of joy and pride, as if their kid were mayor or governor or president giving her inaugural address . . .

The first time a person realizes he or she is going to die, be placed in a box and buried in the earth . . .

The first time I'll see the face of God . . .

A Letter, In Case You Didn't Get Any Mail Today

Dear Sally and Jim,

Merry Christmas and Happy New Year. I know I'm two months late with this letter, but for me, being two months late, hey, that's not bad. In fact, for those who really know me, it's a miracle.

My son Jimmy bought me a computer for Christmas. At first I balked, saying I was computer illiterate. I had all the excuses. Now I'm a computer addict. What an easy way to write letters.

Thank you for your Christmas card and news about the family. I'm glad the two of you are enjoying your retirement in San Diego. I've never been there, but I've always heard that the weather there is perfect 365 days a year. You can't beat that. I hear it never gets very hazy, hot or humid there—and you remember what it feels like around here like in July. Enjoy. Praise God. Both of you deserve it after all the work you did raising those seven wonderful kids of yours. Hope everyone is doing fine. Love to all.

Now for the reason it's taken me so long to answer your Christmas card and note.

I have sad news for you. My Sarah died in November. Sorry I didn't call you. I just wasn't up to it.

I'm okay now. I didn't send Christmas cards because Sarah always did them. She died of a heart attack just before Thanksgiving. I could have called, but it was tough for me at the time, tough seeing so many friends from around here. I just couldn't contact all the people I worked with all those years before retirement, many of whom like you, moved to Florida, California, or Arizona.

Sarah had the heart attack on November 18th. She died in the hospital two days later.

The kids and I were horribly shocked, grieved. Kevin, Jenny, Terry, Paul, Christopher and Molly were there before she died. Claire, who lives in Korea with her husband, didn't make it back in time. She's okay. She made it to the funeral. Thank God we were all together for that sacred moment.

Thank God for kids and grandkids, for family, and for so many wonderful friends. The old gang from around here came to the funeral.

In the hospital, just before she died, Sarah kept fading in and out of consciousness. I think all of us were able to look into those beautiful blue eyes and say, "I love you. Thank you for so much. Thank you for everything."

Gratitude. I feel so much gratitude for such a wonderful woman, such a wonderful friend, wife, mom for our kids. Thank You, Lord.

At the Mass, after Communion, Molly delivered a touching tribute to her mom. Molly always had a great gift for words. I've listened to a tape of the service a dozen times since then and cry every time.

I thank God for our faith. I don't think we could have made it without our faith.

Some days are better than others. Sometimes the waters are calm and sometimes they're a bit choppy. At times there are big, silent waves of loneliness that come crashing over me. Many nights I've slept on the couch, because our bed feels like a deep empty valley. I'm starting a part-time job at the Mall next week, to keep busy. The kids are good. They keep calling, checking on me. I guess they're worried. They invite me to stay with them—to baby sit, just to keep me busy. But as we all tell our kids, "You have your own life to live."

Enough. In fact, I've said too much. These computers can be dangerous. I know that you and Sally would have come to the funeral if you had heard about it. I figured at some point I'd have to go through all these Christmas cards and let all our old friends know what happened.

Thanks again for all the good times we had together at work and those other times we got together for family weddings and this and that through the years. "You're good people," as you always used to say to Sarah and me.

And if I get a chance, I'll get out there to see the two of you and enjoy some of that warm San Diego weather. It's still cold and dreary here. Meanwhile, I'll keep the two of you in my prayers and I'd appreciate yours.

Take care of each other. Enjoy each day and each night you have together. I'm glad Sarah and I did.

Love to both of you from an old friend—but not that old,

Jack

Wanting to be Remembered

"*Do* this in memory of me."

Everyone wants to be remembered.

Kids carve their names on trees, stick their initials into fresh cement, mark their nicknames onto bathroom walls.

Dads try to show up at spelling bees and moms at soccer games.

Old people look at telephones and wait for mail to be delivered.

Children take care of their parents' graves—bringing flowers—pulling weeds from around the stone—the stone that has names and dates chiseled into it.

We are remembered in the telling of family stories or at Thanksgiving or Christmas, when the photo albums come out.

Will I be remembered?

We look around the house and see photographs on the television set or a bedroom dresser. We see trophies with our name on them on a basement shelf. There are letters we've sent to people, some of which might be saved. Our name will someday appear in an obituary column of the local newspaper and on stone in the cemetery.

Paul Tillich said in a sermon, "In the depth of the anxiety of having to die is the anxiety of being eternally forgotten."

Is that true for everyone? Does every person become anxious about death and the possibility of "being eternally forgotten?"

"Kilroy was here." Whoever Kilroy was, he wrote his name everywhere. Do I do the same thing in my own way? Is everything I do simply my graffiti, my way of saying, "I was here. Don't forget me."

Is that why we send postcards from distant places and why we bring home souvenirs?

Am I trying to carve my own tombstone before I die? Am I doing everything that I do in order to be remembered for a few generations?

Or am I trying to tell myself that I'm here? I've been here. My life has meaning. Am I also wondering if my life means anything to the other people in my life?

I look at Jesus—a carpenter who left no children, no furniture, no letters, nothing material. I sometimes wonder whether those who had a chair made by him, or a table, would bring neighbors in and point out, "This was made by Jesus the Carpenter."

Sitting here quietly, I remember Jesus. I look to him and ask him to take away my anxiety.

I pray:

Lord Jesus, you died when you were around thirty-three. You told people not to worry and fret about the little things. Yet when it came to life and death, you were quite serious, weren't you?

The night before you died, you handed the cup to others to drink—the cup of life, the cup of your blood—the cup of your being—being alive—but tomorrow possibly passing over to death.

That night you said, "Do this in memory of me."

But later that night in the garden you hesitated. You had to make a decision about taking the cup. And you took it in memory of me.

I take and drink the cup of life and death in memory of you.

And now in memory of you, I trust in resurrection and life. I won't be forgotten for a thousand generations, or a million, or ever. I know you'll be waiting for me beyond my grave. Like Lazarus, I too will hear your tears and your cry, "Come forth!"

Jesus, you said all these things. I know these words because others remembered them and wrote them down.

When I think of death, I'm anxious, but when I think of you, I'm less afraid. I know you'll be there on the other side of my death. And then there will be eternal embrace, eternal dance, eternal remembering.

The Dance

"*D*ance then wherever you may be: I am the Lord of the Dance, said he."

For some reason, that song, that Shaker hymn, those words, that music started whirling in my mind that day. And I started to dance, started to smile. I found myself walking differently. I skipped. I danced down the sidewalk all the way to work that morning.

Somehow, ever since that day, that song, that smile, that dance, has beat in my heart. It was an eye opener. It was a foot mover. And ever since then, people have asked, "Wow. Why are you always smiling? Why do you always seem to be happy?" And in response, I smile. And ever since then, I've kept on dancing, as I do my work. I keep on dancing, as I live my day.

"Dance then wherever you may be: I am the Lord of the dance, said he."

It's hard to explain. Up until then I could never dance.

"I can't dance." That was my line. My excuse.

At least that's what I always told myself.

So at weddings, I was always one of the sitters, the watchers of the dance, on the edge of the dance floor.

Oh, I've been dragged onto the dance floor by my sisters, by my mother, by others. And each time the same thing happened: my dance partner would say, "You can't dance. You have two left feet." And I'd always say, "I know. That's why I was sitting comfortably till you dragged me out here!"

But now, ever since that morning, the morning when I heard that tune on my way to work, I dance.

And once I started to dance, I discovered that all of life is the dance. All of life, all its steps, are steps of the great dance.

For me, before that, things were out of tune. Everything in life was disconnected. Work. Play. Sleep. Family. Faith. Meetings. This. That. Nothing was connected. I was out of step. No wonder I couldn't dance.

Why?

I don't know.

Maybe until then I thought life was all work and no fun.

Until then I was missing the *all* because I was looking at the *small*.

Or maybe I was too close to myself. Too worried about my "two left feet." I wanted to protect myself from looking foolish. So I spent my life sitting down, being careful, never getting up to dance the dance. So I was missing the music. Not hearing the beat, the Earth's heartbeat. Life.

So I wasn't seeing how all the moments are united, are holding hands, are dancing together in one big connection.

Now I do. Then I didn't. I'm beginning to see that everything is part of the dance. All earth and all its inhabitants are partners in the dance. And Earth and all the planets are swinging around and around the sun and all are partners in the dance. And all the solar systems are swinging around in the great, great dance. And we're dancing in the dark, not knowing where the dance or dance floor ends—if it ever ends. And the dance goes on and on, spinning around in this great universe.

Until that morning, I was "into words." All I heard was words and commands: "Hear the word of your mother, your father, your brother, your sister, your boss, your other." And when I went to church it was to hear words, words, words, all words: "Hear the word of the Lord."

Too often I was like the older brother in the famous story of The Prodigal Son. I was good at work, work, work, but when I came home, I didn't understand the music and dance of life. Thanks to Jesus, I'm finally getting it. Life is family. Life is celebration. Life is a banquet.

The dance goes on. Now I stop to watch clouds glide past the moon and I smile. Now when I see birds flying north in the Spring and south in the Fall, I know it's exactly the reverse in the southern hemisphere, and still the very same dance.

Morning dance: the paper boy tossing the paper, alarms going off, dogs barking, roosters crowing, the shower drumming the sounds of wonderful water on my back, the coffee perking, the toaster popping, the car starting, the flow of traffic, morning patterns, people moving in every direction, cars, buses, trains, planes, all dancing, people moving in all kinds of transportation, different means of communication, and all of this happening everywhere on Earth!

Evening dance: people moving homeward, people stuck in traffic, some not noticing, some going crazy, some listening to traffic reports, others listening to music, wondering what's for supper, wondering what's happening with the rest of the family. All over the world.

Sabbath. Work days. Tearing down. Building up. Buying and selling. Making and taking. Planting and harvesting.

Migration. Movement. Animals mating, foraging, surviving, dying. People going to church, mosque and synagogue.

The lab technician looking into a microscope, observing a cell and studying the dance of life or death.

The astronomer at night looking into a telescope and watching a star shower flooding the universe.

A child twisting a kaleidoscope and seeing everything around her in an ongoing dance of color and light.

Sitting in the stands at the football game watching the plays unfold, athletes running and rushing, crowds cheering . . . Sitting in a high school auditorium, enjoying a musical, watching young people acting out some of the future roles of life . . . Sitting in traffic watching kids get off the yellow bus and rush toward their homes, their kitchens, their refrigerators, their comfortable clothes. And the dance goes on.

"Dance then wherever you may be: I am the Lord of the Dance, said he."

Nobody

Nobody is nobody.

Everybody is somebody.

Everybody has been Somebody to someone sometime.

"Let the good times roll."

Let the bad times stop.

We're not numbers.

We're Somebody—somebody with a name.

As the song goes, "I've Got a Name."

"Emily." What a beautiful name.

Have you ever read Emily Dickinson's poem about being a Nobody? Let's hope everyone in some American Lit class has heard it and reflected on it somewhere along the way.

It's poem # 288. Her poems are without names—just numbers. There are 1775 of them in *The Complete Poems of Emily Dickinson*, edited by Thomas H. Johnson. Poem # 288 was written about 1861.

Listen carefully to her words. You can still hear her, a Somebody named Emily Dickinson.

> "I'm Nobody! Who are you?
>
> Are you—Nobody—Too?
>
> Then there's a pair of us?
>
> Don't tell! they'd advertise—you know!
>
> How dreary—to be—Somebody!
>
> How public—like a Frog —
>
> To tell one's name—the livelong June—
>
> To an admiring Bog!"

Emily was Somebody—somebody with depth, with thoughts and feelings about all sorts of issues that people on this Earth think about and deal with. For example, feeling like a Nobody. She even capitalizes the word: "Nobody." Do you ever feel that way? Critics suppose that she was thinking about fame. Does everyone, at some time or other, think of fame?

Reading her poems today, one can relate with Somebody who lived yesterday, from 1830 to 1886.

During her lifetime, only seven of her poems were published. After her death, all 1775 of her poems were published.

There were days when Emily felt like a Nobody, this woman who wrote poem after poem listening to herself figuring herself out.

She also wrote letters, letter after letter to different people attempting to find out about her poems and her life and their lives. "Are you—Nobody—Too?"

At age thirty-one, she read an article in *The Atlantic Monthly* by Thomas Wentworth Higginson about how young writers can break into print. One of his suggestions was, "Charge your style with life."

So on April 15,1862, she wrote to Higginson—enclosing four of her poems. She asked him if her verses "breathed."

A correspondence began. It lasted for the rest of her life. Somebody writing to Somebody. He saw Life in her verses. He asked for more. They breathed. Still, he didn't recommend publication. He didn't know how to classify them. He once said to a friend that her verses were "remarkable," but "not strong enough to publish."

Lavinia Dickinson, Emily's younger sister, thought differently. Sorting through her sister's possessions after Emily's death, Lavinia found a small box containing about 900 poems. Fortunately, for all of us, she saved them. Then she fought to have them published.

After her death, Emily Dickinson became a Somebody—classified with Walt Whitman as "the two best American poets of the Nineteenth Century."

Does everybody on Earth have something special that nobody seems to notice? Do you? Do I? Is the problem the "aftertaste" of feelings remaining when we are treated like a Nobody?

Does everyone have a Someone in her life—a sister, brother, child, friend,—who will save and sort out their treasures after they have died, because she or he was Somebody for them?

Nobody is a Nobody.

Mother Teresa of Calcutta said, "One of the worst diseases is to be Nobody to Nobody."

I hope you and I have someone to be Somebody to.

A Nun's Story

I'm a nun. You don't know me, so let me tell you something about myself *from the inside.*

In a way, a nun lives a very ordinary life. In another way, it's extraordinary.

Nuns are seen by "outsiders" in four stereotypical ways:

1) Crazy! What a waste!

2) The Good Sister. The Little Nun. Wonderful. Sweet. An Angel.

3) Indifference: Who cares?

4) A sexless, frigid woman.

I live with nuns. We laugh at those caricatures and we laugh at each other. Yet, sometimes, down deep, the stereotypes hurt. We're real. We carry all the baggage that everyone else carries—and most of us have tried to carry less.

I'm thirty-seven, good looking, with red hair, freckles, 5'7," 122 pounds. If I weighed a bit more, you wouldn't be hearing me telling you my weight. See! I'm real.

I started as a grade school teacher—first grade. I loved it. When you don't have kids, it's great to be with them and see them grow. And I'll be honest: sometimes it's good to see them go home to someone else who is their parent.

Things changed when I met Jason. He was a first grader who was deaf. I couldn't reach him. He was stuck in silence. I learned sign language, so I could communicate with him. That's how I got into full time teaching and ministry with the hearing-impaired. During the day I worked with kids. In the evening and on weekends I communicated with adults and kids—in sign language. Fascinating.

Maybe you want to know some of the inside story.

I was about to be married. Tom and I had been going together for two years. He was a lawyer and part-time drummer in a band. I was a business analyst. We were in love, had all kinds of wonderful adventures together, were always on the phone. Our families liked the match. The wedding date was set. We had a hall, had a church, had airline tickets for our honeymoon.

Then suddenly something surfaced from down deep within me. Something was wrong. Something was missing.

We both knew it. Tom sensed it even before I did. I said I needed time. It killed me to see it killing him. But he was a great guy and he gave me space.

He's married now and here I am a nun. Me, a nun! Who would believe it? He went to Catholic schools and never missed Church. I was Catholic "in name only." Never went to church. Okay, I went at Christmas and Easter sometimes. Went to a public school, so I never experienced that going-to-become-a-nun-someday phase. Oh, I was flighty and up-in-the-air as a kid; but becoming a nun wasn't one of my flights of fancy.

And it was up in the air that it happened. I was flying home to Chicago after a business trip. And there she was—a "little old nun"—sitting just across the aisle from me. She was perhaps sixty. On her head she wore a veil and it was lopsided.

When the "Bink! Bink!" sounded telling us we could unfasten our seat belts, she turned her head and faced me for a moment. I suppose she wanted to see where the "Bink! Bink!" was coming from. What a smile. Serenity. Joy. Echoes of peace radiating from her. At least that's what bounced off my eyes and mind in one glance.

I sat and watched her. I had never ever paid attention to a nun before. Nuns were non-existent people to me. She was friendly to the flight attendants and there were two small children in front of me who were cranky. They came over to her. She calmed them down and began joking with them. They were enthralled and she was giving their mom a break.

That simply dressed (but richly endowed) person changed my life. I didn't even speak to her. I found myself watching her during the whole trip to Chicago.

Later, I couldn't get God out of my mind. That nun put God into my thoughts. She helped me to see that it was God I needed. God was missing from my life.

So during lunch time I began going to a small church in downtown Chicago. I walked in and there learned to know God. Our family had dropped out of Church; and here I was dropping into church every day.

And I fell in love with God.

Almost married, I knew what it meant to be "in love": thinking, calling, giving, wanting, wishing, yearning, holding, needing.

Falling in love with God was Phase One.

What next? I could love God and be married. Millions of people do that.

I could love God and have a family, have a career, have a comfortable life. Millions of people are doing that, too.

Decisions.

Who was the nun on the plane? What is her name?

I don't know, but she is Somebody.

And that Somebody in her quiet gentleness, showed me God, and what a life dedicated to God could mean. And the dear man I loved so well understood the grace I'd been given and through tears wished me happiness and peace.

And so I became a nun. That's it. My parents couldn't believe it. They thought I had fallen out of a tree and cracked my head.

But I became a nun, and it became me.

People now see me laughing with kids who can't hear, or see me *signing* a sermon in church for a handful of hearing-impaired people. They see my red hair and freckles and some have said, "Did you every think of marriage?" and I smile. And maybe some think, "What a waste!"

I smile. I believe I could have found God if I had married. I know people who came back to Religion once they've had a child. Yet this is my story. This is the way God found me.

And who knows? Maybe someone someday will see me on a plane, or in church, or playing with kids who can't hear—and they may know God because of me?

With all my heart, I hope so . . .

Everybody
is a Story

Sometimes when someone tells their story, we listen, and as we listen, we hear our own story. "They're playing our song."

Isn't that how it works? Isn't that the secret that story tellers know? Isn't that what movies that move us to laughter and tears do? I see myself on the screen. They're telling my story. Isn't that what happens as we read a novel we can't put down, that we rush to after supper, after every interruption in the day's work?

Stories. Everyone loves a good story. Everybody has a story. Everybody *is* a story. Everybody is a *story book*.

Who reads me?

Who listens to me?

The Earth listens.

The Earth wants life to go on. The Earth wants its story to continue— chapter by chapter, page by page, verse by verse, person by person.

And when people forget to listen to each other, when groups fail to communicate with each other, when tribes and nations don't sit down at the table with each other, the fabric of life is torn apart.

The teenager trembles hearing her parents scream and gradually divorce themselves from each other in the next room. The Seventh Grader gives up after saying to a teacher or coach over and over, "This isn't fair. You're playing favorites." The teacher or coach never asks, "Let's sit down. I want to know what you're talking about, what you're feeling."

We need to find someone to tell our story to—not everyday, but at special moments—to have someone who really listens to us. "It's not good to be alone." (*Genesis 2:18*)

We all need to get whatever we're talking to ourselves about out on the table. We need someone to hear us, to listen to what we're saying—what we're not saying. Someone who knows what we feel, who feels what we feel, who cares about us.

Intimacy is having someone, not everyone, but someone whom we can really talk to—not all the time, but some times. If we meet three such persons before we die, we're blessed. If we think we've been intimate with many people already, chances are we haven't.

Now of course, in general, women are better at intimacy than men. John Gray's book, *Men Are From Mars, Women Are From Venus,* states this clearly. Get a stop watch and see how long men talk to men on the telephone—then time the women. We all know relationships would improve 100 percent if people really listened to each other.

Listening gives life—to the listener and to the one listened to.

Has anyone ever heard the story of *my* life? Have I ever *told* it?

I once had a small cut on my finger. I rarely use Band-Aids for cuts like that, but I did this time. I was sitting at a family gathering and from the other side of the room my grandnephew, Christopher, spotted my cut. He came over, pointed at the Band-Aid and said, "Hurt? What happened?"

"What happened?"

What a perfect question! It's the leading question for class reunions. It's the question behind the dinner-time question, "How was your day?"

"How is your *life?*"

I once heard a speaker say that Americans are nomads. The first question we ask each other is, "Where do you come from?"

Each person, every family, each organization and every town, church, temple and mosque, has its "Origins," its "Genesis" story, its "Where do you come from?" story.

One of my favorite TV programs is *Booknotes*. I try to catch it on Sunday evenings. No commercials. Brian Lamb is an excellent interviewer. He listens. The format is simple: a person sitting down talking to another person—usually someone who has just written a book. Brian Lamb asks "Origins" questions to the person he interviews and then gets out of the way. It's not by accident that question marks are shaped in the form of a hook:

"What got you started writing?"

"Where do you come from?"

"Your Mom and Dad?"

"Any brothers or sisters?"

"When do you write?"

"What got you off on this?"

"Any surprises, discoveries, while you were writing this?"

"Any surprises, discoveries, after your book was published?"

Haven't we often been at a funeral when a member of the family gets up and gives a wonderful eulogy? I sometimes watch people in the benches and not the speaker. When someone who didn't know the deceased preaches, I often see people glancing at their watches, prayer books, statues, and stained glass windows. But when a son or a daughter speaks about their Dad or Mom, brother or sister, everyone stares directly at the speaker. And later at the cemetery or luncheon, I hear people speaking about the eulogy. "Wasn't that wonderful?" "What a marvelous tribute." "It was so personal." "I never knew that about him (or her)."

Why do we wait till someone dies to hear their story? Turn off the TV and listen. Get out the old photos and find out, "Who's who?" and "What's what?" and "Where's that?" Jot down the answers on a label pasted on the back of each photo, so you can tell the story to those who follow you on the family tree.

Everybody has a story.

Everybody is a story.

My life: Good days? Bad days? Ups and downs? Falls from grace? Hitting bottom? Risings? Resurrection from the dust? Starting again and again?

My story: Who's listening to my story? Who's opening and reading the pages of my life?

Maybe others would listen to me more, if I listened to myself more. And a good way to begin doing this is to discover the incidents of my life mirrored in the pages of the Bible.

In *Nelson's Complete Concordance of the New American Bible,* I looked up the words, "listen" and "hear." "Listen" is used 272 times and "hear" is used 402 times. Have we ever counted up in a day how many times people use these two words, "listen" and "hear"? Reading, listening and hearing Bible stories, we have an opportunity to hear about the great issues of life, and then to ponder, and discover our own lives throughout the Bible.

The Bible is essentially a collection of stories that helps us hear our own stories. Stories connect stories.

Everyone needs stories, movies, plays, newspapers, sitting and listening to each other, in order to see how the story of one's own life is unfolding.

We are many-colored threads going north and south, east and west, becoming whole cloth, becoming whole.

The story of Adam and Eve helps us get to the beginning of things.

The story of Abraham and Sarah helps us understand the times in our life when we moved from security to insecurity, from one city to the next, from one country to another, from light to darkness—times we made a move—took a chance—risked—made leaps of faith.

The story of Joseph helps us understand family feuds, jealousy, tragedy, and that good can come out of evil—if only we dream, if only we forgive, if only we understand.

The story of Moses helps us get in touch with the times we were stuck—addicted—trapped—and needed help.

Life is movement across seas, deserts, rivers, hoping to find Promised Land. Life is fighting giants and armies, choosing leaders, choosing God. Life is a love story and sometimes a betrayal story. Life is a long story of people going on and on . . .

Who's listening?

Sitting Under a Tree

Taking the time to sit under a tree, to relax, to do nothing, then beginning to think, to ponder, to pray . . .

God, it's been a long day. It's been a long life.

Adam died a year ago today.

Do men die first? Do women deal with death better than men? Do birth pains in bringing a child into this world, with its stretching of physical and emotional energies, help someone to deal better with the birth pains of death?

I don't know.

When Cain killed Abel, I'm not sure which of us was devastated more. Adam was not good with feelings—especially after we lost Paradise.

He blamed me for that. He always did.

Being on our own, outside the garden of our beginnings, was quite a struggle: work, children, questions, too many questions of what might have been.

Sin: the fall from grace. The loss of innocence. The aftertaste of biting into forbidden fruit.

Sin? Grace? Which one is the better teacher?

Sitting under a tree, wondering if God knew we would eventually eat from the tree of the knowledge of good and evil.

Sin. Stupidity. Death.

It was our "NO" to God's way that changed everything.

I still don't know the "WHY?"

Why did we do it? Can sin ever be the best thing that ever happened to us? We were mere children in the Garden. We didn't have to work. We didn't have to make decisions. Everything was handed to us.

I suppose in time everyone gets the itch to be out from under those above us, to be our own boss—our own god, wanting our own way—at least to try it?

Well, our choice got us out on our own.

I guess that's another aftertaste of sin—the slow realization that decisions and actions have repercussions.

Sin makes me feel so alone.

Sin is so tricky. Sometimes it sneaks up like a snake. It whispers only good. It promises new growth, new power, new freedom. It hides its consequences of death, decay and dependence.

And then we want to crawl away, to hide in the undergrowth.

Was it better that we fell?

The devil was right. That day we learned knowledge of good and evil.

The devil also lied. We tasted death that day—and we grind our teeth with death's bad breath ever so many days afterwards.

God, it was our choice to eat the forbidden fruit.

And, God, when we did, we became less and less your image.

Sin . . . Sin became our image.

Sometimes sin seems so right on the surface, so bright, like the shiny skin of a rotten apple. Then when we bite into it, we immediately want to spit it out.

But sometimes sin is a slow poison—a seeping cancer—that takes years of ups and downs to finally figure some of it out. It has become us. We have digested too much sin.

So, God, here I am still figuring the ins and outs of temptation, sin, life, and death. Here I am sitting under my own tree eating from the fruit of my own knowledge of good and evil.

Asking questions seems to be an important step in life.

Looking back seems to be another. And looking back, I suppose a fall can be one of the best ways to rise.

Listening to you seems to be the secret.

God, did you tell us about the tree of choices because that is the only way we could be free?

We need to talk about this—sitting here together under this tree. I need to hear your footsteps again, to feel your presence in the cool breeze of evening.

God, I am sitting here, waiting for you. It's good. This time I don't have to hide.

Summer Nights
&
Ice Cream Cones

On a summer night, everyone loves to go for ice cream.

Two boys, one seven, the other nine, stood there that hot summer night eating their ice cream cones. The ice cream was leaking fast. They were experiencing a meltdown. The boys were finally "grown up": Mom and dad gave them total control over the choice of what flavors their two scoops of ice cream could be.

Dad always chose two scoops of vanilla. Cone in hand, he loved to step back to observe the scene. "Great ice cream. Great wife. Great kids. Could anyone be in a better place, on a clear summer night, than the parking lot of 'Ice Cream Delight'?" He was at peace. Ice cream can do that. Inwardly he was also thinking, "These last four months at work have been too stressful. Thank God, the project is finally over. The orders are all filled. Things will slow down now—at least till September."

Mom was more flamboyant. Maybe that's why they married each other. They were "order" and "disorder," vanilla and thirty-seven different flavors. She stood there enjoying the taste of chocolate-chocolate chip. And that was just the top scoop. Underneath was her second scoop: raspberry sherbet-twirl with raisins! The kids loved this about their mom: she ordered different flavors every time. And she always ordered last. She loved surprises, last-minute, spur-of-the-moment choices. She knew her sons stood there waiting to hear her choices at the sliding window.

Mom was smiling "big time." She was enjoying the summer night sky. Summer. Vacation. Her boys. Her husband. But she also loved September when the house returned to quiet with the boys back in school. She had a computer and was back to writing while the boys were at school and her husband was at work.

Back to the boys.

One stood there, delighting in his pistachio and peach cone. He too enjoyed the night sky. And after each twirling lick of his ice cream, he would close his eyes. He loved to feel the cold ice cream against his teeth and tongue and then to feel it slide down his throat heading for his tummy.

His brother wasn't happy. He usually wasn't. He was hardly tasting his ice cream. Once more, he felt that he made the wrong choices. Seeing the delight on his brother's face, he was wishing he too had gotten pistachio and peach. And it dug deeper into his pain, especially when his Dad said to his brother, "You really seem to be enjoying that!"

"Yeah, dad, I really am. U-m-m-m good!"

And that's the way the four of them were for the rest of their lives.

So Many Voices,
So Many Choices

In the Foreword to his play, *After The Fall*, Arthur Miller wrote, "Where choice begins, Paradise ends, innocence ends, for what is Paradise but the absence of any need to choose this action?"

What makes us human?

Is it hearing these inner and outer voices and having to make so many choices?

Is it the end of innocence and the loss of Paradise?

Is it freedom to choose this action and not that one?

Or is it thinking? Feeling? Forgiving? Remembering? Is it celebrating anniversaries? Laughter? Prayer? Kindness? Is it taking care of our elderly?

Or is it making pots and pans, carving statues and drawing pictures on the walls of our caves? Is it making machinery, playing with dolls and creating classrooms and religious centers?

Is it being able to abstract, to figure, to hunger for meaning, for answers to our questioning?

Is it knowing that I can lose my soul before I die and before I die I can rise from inner death?

Or is all of the above? Is it seeing the connections between all choices, seeing that all is one, and that all is one because this is God's choice?

What makes us human?

So many voices, so many choices . . .

Is the key to being human this ability of ours to make choices, to choose good or evil?

Is it this coming out of the paradise of childhood, discovering that we can make decisions, some of which go against the voice of God, choosing evil, losing our innocence, discovering that we or others can be cruel and harm one another?

I wonder.

Owls, leopards, lions and laboratory mice choose?

What makes us human?

In the beginning of the Bible, we read about the first man and woman being given the gift of choice. All was good till they had to decide whether to eat the fruit from the tree of the knowledge of good and evil?

We humans know very well that we can choose good or evil.

To be conscious of that choice: Is that what makes us human?

To become more and more conscious of the voices within us, one saying that everything God creates is good and another voice, a rebellious itch, that wants something to be recreated for our image and likeness: Is that what makes us human?

Good and evil . . . God's way and my way . . . Walking with God or walking alone . . . Choices . . . Voices . . .

So is the answer that Micah the Old Testament prophet said, "You have been told what is good and what the Lord requires of you. Do only what is right. Love goodness. Walk humbly with your God."

To be good or not to be good?

To use or misuse the gifts of God?

To spread gossip or to keep quiet and not further damage another's reputation?

To tell the secret or to keep it?

To love or to lust?

To take a creative risk or to sit back and stagnate doing the same old thing day after day after day?

To tailgate, to beep, to curse, or to calmly stay a few car lengths back behind a car we can't pass?

To avoid those who bore us at every coffee break or to actually listen to them without having our eyes on the other side of the room?

To be a prophet and speak out for justice or to disappear and let injustice have the day and the night?

To pick up litter and beautify the path or to be one of those who litter?

To listen to another and to ask follow up questions, or to jump in as soon as the other person pauses to take a breath?

To choose to turn off the TV, to become quiet, to pray, to reflect upon the options we have, to choose the good, then to do the good, to walk humbly with our God.

To be able to choose or not to choose: Is that what makes us human?

What makes us human?

Is it this streak in us to be inhuman, to be selfish, to cause hell for others instead of working together to regain Paradise? Is that what makes us human?

Or is it final realization that we are not Divine and that the Divine became human so that we can become Divine?

I hope so.

I believe so.

I know so, sometimes.

Astronaut

As a boy, I always wanted to fly, to leap off stoops, steps, stairs, chairs, desks, tables, anything that was higher than I was. Oh, I also wanted to be a basketball player, a baseball player, a trombone player and one of the kids who could leap from the high diving board.

But an astronaut: to be an astronaut? No. I never had that dream as a boy. I was born before the Space Age. But when space ships started to orbit around the earth, dreams began.

Wasn't it those pictures shot from outer space—pictures taken from space-craft windows—that gave us the dream that we too would love to be up there? Who didn't stare at the television screen when Planet Earth was pictured from way out there in Space?

Compared to those light blue globes in our classrooms, with all that tiny writing on them, with countries divided, and given different colors, this was real. This was live and in living color—our Earth. To see the round globe of Earth from outer space—way down there, a spinning marble—glass like in the light—green, blue, mostly blue, some gray, some black, streams and rivers blending colors, and then snow white tips on top and bottom, all this was awesome—this, our Earth, in soothing watercolors.

Thanks to the astronauts and their cameras we could see ourselves in a new way. We had a new picture of planet Earth. A new viewpoint. The astronauts looked out the window and saw so much differently. Their cameras gave us a sense of wonder—a sense of awe on seeing it all.

Seeing no human boundaries, just nature's. Learning that we are just one world. That we are all in this together—together with the waters and the land, the mountains and the gulfs. That we humans are very small compared to oceans and seas and continents. Seeing this *big picture,* we can develop a sense of perspective about ourselves in the overall scheme of things.

When astronauts orbit the Earth for the first time, do they find themselves spending their time looking out the window? Is time for wonder built into their schedules or do they have to get to work right away?

To be an astronaut is to be one of a select few. What about the rest of us? How do we see the Earth? Do we have a sense of wonder from here below?

Come to think of it, don't we all know people who have never lost their sense of wonder? They still have children's eyes. We see them in the mall enjoying people walking by—waving and saying, "Hi" as they look others in the eye. We see them at parties and picnics—just observing—just smiling—just taking it all in.

Some see these people as "out of it"—"space cadets"—"flighty"—"astronauts."

I see them as alive—gifted with a child's sense of wonder.

I see this gift in those I call "window people"—people who love to look out windows: people who park themselves with folded arms to watch the street on a summer's evening; people sitting there in the morning, in the quiet kitchen, with a cup of coffee watching the sun rise on the leaves and birds in their backyard; people alone in a restaurant near a front window, watching couples and families come to the front door and seeing who holds the door open for whom; people pulling back their curtains to look out a window late at night right before going to bed, watching backyard branches scratching the surface of the moon.

A sense of wonder. A touch of the poet in everyone.

Don't we spend too many hours looking at nothing worthwhile in the television window—forgetting about the live world and the live people all around us?

And now for recreation some of us are spending too much time looking into computer screens—opening and closing windows. As one bishop put it, "I wish some of my priests would interface with people more than computer screens."

Window people.

I'm a window person myself—always wanting the window seat on planes, trains and buses.

Aisle seats? I think they are for people who are "in a hurry"—even aisle seats in a bus.

I remember two wonderful bus trips to Portland, Maine, with my Dad when I was a boy. He gave me the window seat. It was like being an astronaut before there were astronauts. I sat high up there, looking down at our world from a bus window. To a kid a bus can be as good as a spaceship.

Finally the doors would close. The lights would go off for a moment. The motor would rev up. And then we would blast off—pulling out of the big bus station in New York City. There we were rolling out of the depot, seeing the street in the early morning light, watching people sitting in doorways staring at the ground, men walking along, shuffling and greeting each other as if they were sleep-walking, dazed from alcohol, in a stupor.

Pointing, I asked my dad, "Who are those men?"

"Men out of work, I guess. And last night they probably drank too much."

"Oh!" And I sat there wondering about those men? Were they Dads? Did they have kids? Could this ever happen to my Dad? Could this ever happen to me?

Years later, I would say, "No!" Much later I learned to say, "There but for the grace of God go I."

In the Lincoln Tunnel, our bus suddenly became a submarine. That's how I pictured it when my Dad told me that we were now under water. I was a bit scared seeing so many tiles all the way to the other side. What if one broke?

Out of the Lincoln Tunnel, into another state: New Jersey. Soon we were rolling—still high above the cars—wondering what it would be like to be in a car. We never had one. We grew up traveling in trolleys, buses and subway trains.

On each of those trips with my Dad, I was as good as an astronaut, seeing a whole new world, from "way up there," looking out bus windows: seeing trees, hills, and then the mountains—the first time I saw mountains was from the window of a bus.

I still thank my Dad and all others who take the aisle seat. Window seats have kept the poet alive in me. I see life as a bus ride—many stops along the way—all of us moving forward in time toward the journey's end. Some try to do life alone or with a select few, like those in the cars below. I prefer to go it with a group—like on a bus—like on a plane—like an astronaut—all of us dependent on others to keep us going.

We're connected, interconnected, all of us here on Earth. We need each other. We are like astronauts, spinning around and around in space on Spaceship Earth. We have only so much oxygen, water, and supplies for the trip.

So I suppose the more we look out windows, the more we'll realize the need to take care of Spaceship Earth. We'll see the need to be better planners and organizers of what we have for ourselves as well as for tomorrow's children.

Yesterday

Just yesterday, it all began.

Genesis . . .

In the beginning it began and what began is still beginning.

And all is good . . .

Yesterday is still happening today . . .

Patterns: there are only so many patterns and then we begin to repeat ourselves.

Genesis is still going on.

The book is still being written.

God is still in the process of sculpting all these great works of art that surround us here on Earth. God's Spirit is still hovering over the deep waters. God is still calling into the dark night, "Let there be light."

And there *is* light and there are days—yesterdays and days like today.

And God sees that light is better than darkness.

And all is good . . .

God is still creating the Heavens and the Earth—the waters above and the waters below—still separating the oceans from the land—still seeing that all is good.

God is still creating the plants and the trees, the birds of the air and the fishes of the sea, and the animals that crawl and move along the paths of the earth.

And God is still forming us from the clay of Mother Earth and that is good. It's good to be alive—yesterday and today and tomorrow. And God is still telling us, "Be fruitful and multiply and fill the earth." And sex is good. And children are good. And life is good.

And God is good.

God? How else can we account for all the goodness that is around us, yesterday and today and tomorrow?

We have eyes that see, ears that hear, hands that touch, noses that smell, a mouth that can taste, all the goodness of our Earth, the goodness of our God.

We have microscopes and telescopes and all kinds of devices that can detect and tell us the story about how the Earth and all the life around us is still evolving, still growing, still in progress, yesterday and today and tomorrow.

And our minds keep trying to figure out the story.

Every culture and people have accounts about life on this Earth as they know it—stories, myths, fables, attempts in word and picture, dance and gesture, songs and poems,—that try to explain *yesterday*. These account for origins and mysteries, animals and humans, women and men, good and evil, sin and grace, everything that has been up to now.

How did we get here?

The Ibo and the Egyptians, the Norse and the Navajo, the Chinese and the Greeks, the Hindus and the Mayans, all have their "Genesis" account.

Beginnings . . . Like the Jewish book of Genesis, they were all written yesterday to try to explain today.

Take and read.

Unroll the scrolls.

Listen to the songs.

Watch the dance.

And/or we can slowly put together our own creation story—our own account about what happened yesterday to bring us to today.

All we have to do is open our minds and imaginations as we see creation unfolding: Spring, Summer, Autumn, Winter—year after year after year.

Or we can read the morning paper or watch the evening news. There we'll see the same story that we hear in the first Book of the Bible, Genesis, as well as in the different Origin Stories from other religions and cultures.

The book of Genesis is a good story. It explains our origins very well.

In the beginning all is good. Like parents of a newborn baby wanting everything to be perfect, the authors of Genesis tell of God creating everything to be "just right." It's Paradise. And all is good.

And like every good story, after the opening scene is set, the plot thickens. If we're going to hear about goodness, we have to hear about evil. Light needs to fight darkness—and win—otherwise we won't appreciate the light. Sin collides with grace. People yawn or switch the channel or put down the book, if the story teller doesn't bring in a surprise struggle on every other page. So Genesis has trouble sneak up like a snake in the grass. Or people babble about trying to build a tower that can reach the heavens. How about a really big flood? How about someone being asked to sacrifice a son?

Stories won't grab us and hold us, unless we hear about twists and turns, tests and temptations. Watch kids play video games. Every other moment, there is a threat and a danger that comes flying out of nowhere. Struggle is the name of the game.

Isn't that the story of our life? Of yesterday? Isn't it today? Maybe the phone will ring in five minutes and our life will be changed? Isn't that the excitement of the game?

And that is why everyone "gets" the stories they find Genesis. They are *our* stories. We've all heard the voice of the snake tempting us to taste forbidden fruit: the shiny coin, the chocolate chip cookie, the kiss that betrays.

I exist, therefore, I think, sometimes.

I think about what happened yesterday in order to understand today and tomorrow. We spend most of our awake moments talking to ourselves about what has happened to us. We sometimes wake up in the middle of a strange dream and then spend energy trying to figure what the dream meant.

The people in the book of Genesis do all that. This evening, as we look at our day, we think about what happened to us at home, work, school, playground. We see rivalry and jealousy. We see scenes of brother fighting brother, sister against sister. We can relate to the stories in Genesis about Cain and Abel, Esau and Jacob, Rachel and Leah, Joseph and his brothers.

Our newspapers, novels, movies, Creation accounts—all have the ingredients of what we might have to face each day: temptation, rejection, babble, floods, the need to move, promises, in-laws, deception, sacrifice, disasters that can end up being "the best thing that ever happened to me."

I didn't know that yesterday, but I do know it today.

Balloons

We were just walking, talking, doing nothing but catching up—not expecting to see what we saw when we came around a corner on that day, in a quiet Brooklyn neighborhood.

I was with Tom, a classmate and old friend, whom I hadn't seen in two years. He lived and worked in Santo Domingo; I lived and worked in upstate New York at the time.

We turned the corner and there they were: about 500 school kids, holding 500 balloons of varying colors in their school yard. Excitement, electricity, energy was in the air. Their principal was calling out last-minute instructions over a bull horn.

Parents, lots of parents, grandparents, and people like us stopped and stood there to take in this unique event. The air was crisp and cool; it was March and windy. It was like being at Kennedy Space Center in Florida right before a blast-off.

Talking to parents watching through the black metal fence, we learned that the name of the child, the school, and a message was on the string of each balloon. Why didn't we do this when we were kids? On second thought: I would probably have cheated and sent my name and message to a cousin in Ireland and put a duplicate copy of the message on my balloon and then claimed my balloon went the farthest. Tom said, "I'm flying back to Santo

Domingo tomorrow. Maybe we'll find a balloon around the corner and I'll write back to the kid that I discovered it in Santo Domingo."

Messages in balloons. Messages in bottles tossed into the sea. Messages put in time capsules and sent into space or buried under a new building or underground hoping to say something to someone far away and far into the future.

The moment came.

We were close to the Verrazano bridge where every October some thirty thousand runners from around the world take off for the New York Marathon. The balloons shot off into the sky like runners in a race. They were like Frisbees, red, yellow, green, blue, white balloons flying skyward, with their string tailing them.

The kids screamed, jumped, jubilated, pointed, looked for their parents watching them through the black iron fence. The balloons kept swimming upward like fish in a tank rushing upward when food is spread on the water.

Childhood memories, moments that will fly a long, long time into the deep skies of a child, a person's inner universe.

Looking back, years later, how many of those kids will say, "I remember a day when we all let go of balloons and they went flying upward and outward with our messages into the world?"

Upward and outward. Days ahead. Years ahead. Messages. Leaving home. Parents saying good-bye to their kids at an airport, or as the car pulls out from their driveway, as they leave for college or marriage or a job in a distant city.

Messages. "I got your message." Connections. Reconnections from a distance.

Talking with strangers. Meeting friends. Asking questions.

I don't recall what Tom and I talked about that day, but I'll always remember the moment those balloons took off into the sky.

And from time to time Tom and I send messages, like balloons, back and forth to each other, connecting and reconnecting.

Wheelchair Prayer

*J*udy is a part-time writer and a full-time Mom. BC (Before Children), she was a full-time reporter, a good one. But she discovered that being a full-time Mom was better—much better. Maybe, after the four kids are all in school, she'll return to her newspaper career.

Writing is one of those things you can do whenever you have time and anywhere you find space and on any topic you want to write about.

Besides a magazine article now and then, Judy writes a monthly prayer for a Christian magazine. She composes short prayers on topics and issues like hope, gratitude, suffering, pregnancy, dreams, peace, etc. Everyday scenes set the stage for her everyday prayers.

Like the day she was at a garage sale. She had seen a StepShaper in a friend's house, tried it, was exhausted, but because her friend was so fit, Judy said, "I'm going to start saving money and buy myself a StepShaper."

"Are you crazy?" her friend Jean blurted out. "Just go to garage sales. You'll find one for about $25, and it will probably have only been used once."

"You're kidding!"

"No, I'm serious. People buy all kinds of things, especially exercise equipment, and never use them. Some people don't even take them out of the box. Many give up because they can't understand the 'how to assemble' instructions!"

So that's how Judy ended up at this garage sale. Going around to lots of them looking for a StepShaper, she was also thinking that "exercise" or "going to garage sales" might be a good theme for her monthly prayer.

And there, on that day, she saw it: nice and new and shiny. But it wasn't a StepShaper; it was a *wheelchair*. Almost brand new. It stood next to a card table that had two old toasters on it, a stack of 45-inch records, a pile of old *Popular Mechanic's* magazines, and lots of fishing equipment. "Show me your garage sale," thought Judy, "and I'll tell you who you are. I must write an article on garage sales one of these days."

She bought the wheelchair for twenty dollars. "You never know, someday we might need one."

Her husband, seeing it in the garage, as he got out of the car, came rushing into the house, "What's with the wheelchair? Is one of the kids hurt?"

"Oh, that," Judy said, "I got a good buy on it at a garage sale."

"But *who's* going to use it?"

"You never know. One of these days, one of us, or one of the kids or one of our neighbors or someone in the family, will be looking for a wheelchair. Now we have one."

"Honey, I guarantee you that your wheelchair will remain in our garage with all the other junk we have out there, till we have our own garage sale."

"Maybe," quipped Judy, "and maybe not."

It was near the end of the month and Judy had to write her monthly prayer. "On what?" she wondered. "On what?"

Then the wheelchair came to mind.

"Yes, of course!" thought Judy.

It was her method to write late at night and early in the morning when her husband and the kids were still asleep. She began jotting down leads:

> What would it be like to be in an accident and become paralyzed from the waist down?

> What does the world look like from the seat of a wheelchair?

> How smooth is the ride?

> What's it like being in a wheelchair getting in and out of cars, churches, stores, our house?

An inspiration came.

At breakfast, she asked her husband, "Jim, I need you to take me in my wheelchair to the mall on Saturday, to church on Sunday, and to the high school football game this Friday night."

"You're kidding!"

"No, I want to write a prayer on what it's like looking at life from a wheelchair."

"You're not kidding." Jim knew his wife.

"Well, what will people say? What will you tell people whom we know and who ask, 'What happened?'"

"Simple," said Judy. "I'll just put an Ace Bandage around my ankle and foot and you and the kids will push me around and everyone will think I sprained my ankle."

"You sprained your brain," said Jim laughing.

"No, I'm serious."

So that weekend Judy went everywhere in her wheelchair. Jim loved it. The kids loved it. Judy loved it. Some people asked, "What happened?" Others held doors open for her. To some nothing seemed different.

By Sunday night Judy had enough material for her prayer and this is what she wrote:

WHEELCHAIR PRAYER

Lord,
it's a long and bumpy road,
riding around in this wobbly wheelchair,
hitting doorways, tables, even people,
discovering over and over again,
too many places have no ramp,
no elevator, only stairs.

Lord,
it's a strain and a pain in the neck,
always having to look up to people,
some of whom look down on me,
sometimes because I can't walk,
sometimes because I'm an inconvenience,
and sometimes, maybe they're afraid
that this might happen to them some day.

So Lord,
I guess these are my
stations of the cross:
someone ignoring me,
someone feeling like they are forced to help me,
someone thinking I can't do anything by myself,
feeling trapped or sorry for myself,
but Lord, bathrooms are always
the most difficult stations of them all. Amen.

The Law of Gravity

The law of gravity is quite simple: Someday I am going to be put in a grave and that makes people quite serious.

It's a universal law. Graves make us grave. Death makes us serious.

There is an Italian proverb: "All criminals turn preachers when they are under the gallows."

"There are no atheists in fox holes."

Time.

I have only so much time.

Life. The amazing in between. And then death.

Isn't that the simple, but profound scenario?

Death wears a watch.

Death teaches us about time.

Death makes us hurry—sometimes.

Sometimes it makes us give up. What's the use? Time is running out.

Sometimes it makes us grow up—wake up—change—repent.

A farmer had a great harvest. "What do I do now? Okay. I know what I'll do. I'll tear down that barn, that barn, and that barn. Then I'll build bigger ones. Then I'll have plenty for tomorrow." And Jesus said, "The poor fool doesn't know he's going to die tonight." (*Luke 12:16-21.*)

It ain't fair.

Death is never fair.

As Cervantes put it, "Death eats up all things, both the young lamb and the old sheep."

So the reality of death eats us up and wears us out. It's a loaded gun pointed at our head. Better: It's a time bomb under our seat, under our feet, that's ticking away. Be careful! Someday it will explode and that will be the end of life as we know it.

The law of gravity is not just knowing that death is going to happen someday. It's *realizing* it. That's what gets us. That's what gets us every time.

The law of gravity is simple: Just as we have a birthday, so too we have a deathday. Just as we have a birthday and a card with our name on it: born—8 pounds 3 ounces—so too we have a deathday and a card with our name on it. Our family and friends will pick one up, say the prayer on it, at the time they come to be with each other when our body is laid out in a funeral home.

Timing is everything.

When we are young and someone young dies, it's a shock. It's like a rock thrown through our window. "This is not supposed to happen. It isn't fair." Deeper we're saying, "This could happen to me. I haven't really lived yet."

"The idea of having to die without having lived is unbearable."
(*Erich Fromm*)

When we are old and someone old dies, it's like a rock thrown into a pond. Its ripples hit us.

Death always does something to us.

Death wipes us out. Death always walks along with fear into our house. When someone we know dies, young, old, or in-between, we are shaken. Fears start snaking around inside us, twisting us up for weeks and weeks.

Death: the law of gravity. Another's death makes me serious. The news, the going to the funeral home to give our "love and prayers," the funeral service, being in a funeral procession, the trip to the cemetery, standing at the grave . . . Each of these moments forces us to face the reality that I too will be put in a ground someday.

And all this makes us *grave*.

The apple falls downward from the tree. We are all getting older and gradually hunching our way back to earth.

Another's death impresses us to be grave. Cancer, a heart attack, an accident, remind us that we're all traveling on the path from birth to death.

Most often we live the law of levity, till death knocks on the door of our consciousness, or there's a phone call in the night.

Moses:
Making an Exit

*M*y name is Moses.

Good thing I'm not one of those persons who tries to figure out everything beforehand. I'm not saying that I don't plan. Obviously, planning helps. It's smart to make a list before you go to the market. And I'm not saying I don't have good instincts. What I'm trying to say is this: you can't sit down today and map out what's going to happen tomorrow, that is, *everything* that is supposed to happen tomorrow. It rarely happens that way. Everyone knows their life doesn't turn out the way they planned it.

Right? So we both agree on that. Okay? Now let's get to the reason why you came to see me. What you're asking me to do is to tell you what really happened, so you can write it down. Correct?

Okay, now where do we begin? The beginning or the end? I'm not sure. I'm getting old and when you reach my age, memory starts to play tricks on you. At least mine does. The beginning or the end?

Here I am close to death and we still haven't arrived at the Promised Land. We tried, but we haven't made it yet. And I promised everyone that's what they would get: Promised Land.

It was the hope of a Promised Land that got these people to exit Egypt with me. No group is going to make an exodus like we did, unless they can picture what they are going to receive. A good preacher, a good sales person, has to sell pictures. So I sold them a land flowing with milk and honey. The known is stronger than the unknown. People stay stuck, addicted, even slaves, unless you convince them that there's a much better deal around the corner. So I promised paradise. Land. Their own land. And most people bought the idea. Of course, forced labor, hard work, the whip, as well as those in power trying to keep our population down certainly helped me to get my people moving.

Me? I wasn't a slave. I wasn't in their boat. I was on the opposite shore. I had everything, that is, till I blew it. I killed someone. Back then I had a terrible temper. I have mellowed. The surprise twists and unexpected turns of life have changed me. But when I was young, I could get angry! It might have come from being brought up spoiled. I don't know.

Anyway, I was out walking one day. I turned a corner and I saw an Egyptian beating one of my people, a Hebrew. For a moment, I stood there looking at what was happening. It wasn't fair. The eternal pattern: the big guy picking on the little guy; the have's lording it over the have not's. I lost it. I didn't plan to lose it. I just lost it. I ended up fighting the man. I killed him. Then I panicked and buried his body in the sand.

A moment of passion, a moment of anger, one mistake, and my whole life changed. How many people down through the centuries have lost it all because of one mistake?

The next day, I was walking in the same neighborhood. Dumb? Right. This time I saw two of my own people fighting each other. Why do people always have to be fighting? I tried to stop them—especially the man who was obviously in the wrong. And he fired back at me, "Who said you're in charge? Who made you our judge? Are you going to kill me like you killed the Egyptian?"

Whoa! Can any of us get away with anything? His words hit home. "What do I do now? I'm a marked man." I ran. I'm impulsive, so I ran to get out of town as fast as possible.

I headed for the hills—with nothing, no plan, no clue, no idea about what I was going to do next. One day I had everything; the next day I had nothing. I had been a prince; now I was a pauper.

So now you understand why I said, "You can't plan your life. You never know what's going to happen the next day or the next moment."

I'm sure you've heard my story many times—how I was brought up by the Pharaoh's daughter. She saved me when I was a baby. The order was, "All new Hebrew baby boys must be killed." How could a mother kill her baby? Many mothers did all kinds of things to save their sons. My mother and my sister were very clever. It's one of those bathing scenes you see in plays. They found out where and at what time the Pharaoh's daughter came down to the river with her maids to bathe. My sister waited in the bushes with me in a waterproof basket. Then when the Pharaoh's daughter went into the water to wash, my sister floated me toward her in the basket. A baby floating on the waters. A miracle. How could anyone kill a baby? I was saved, saved by the Pharaoh's daughter.

I never heard how she explained all this to her father, but she was able to pull it off. Here I am.

My mom and my sister didn't stop there. My mom got a job as my nurse. Now being a baby then and being a "hero" now, I don't know how much of the story has slipped into folklore and all that, but that's what they told me. All I know is this: I "had it made" growing up. My people didn't. I was taught how to read and write. Most people didn't have opportunities like that. At least *my* people didn't.

So there I was up in the hills hiding. And it was up in those hills that I really grew up. I became a shepherd, married and started a family of my own.

I figured that was it. I thought that was going to be my life. After living in a palace, it took me a while to adjust to living in a hut or a cave or in the fields, but my wife and family made it worthwhile. I was free.

But my people weren't.

And that's when God called me. I was there minding my own business when God entered my life—in a big way.

God? I grew up hearing about all kinds of gods and goddesses, so I really didn't know about God in capital letters.

God? Even the Pharaoh was seen as a god. I knew he wasn't. I lived with him. I know he acted like one at times. But he knew he was going to die. Aren't wrinkles handwriting on the walls of our skin telling us that our bodies aren't going to last forever? So he chose monuments, big building projects, that would ensure him immortality. He certainly had an "edifice complex." So he was spending lots of money and using my people to build monuments to himself. That is, till God chose us to be to this ongoing city called, "God's Chosen People."

What is life all about? Is it: "Do this in memory of me?" or rather "Do this in memory of someone *greater* than me?"

So God called me. Someone called "God" called *me*.

When I asked for a name, the answer was simply, "I AM"—in Hebrew, "YAHWEH"—I AM WHO I AM is calling you."

God? Experiencing God? I was experiencing God.

Have you ever been out walking in the evening and looked up into the night sky and saw the moon when it's full? Did you stand there amazed at its light and its form? Have you seen spectacular sunsets? Have you studied a baby's fingers and said, "It's a miracle. Five fingers—five beautiful fingers on each hand—and they move."

Well, it happened one day when I was out shepherding. I was heading west. It was late afternoon and I noticed this bush. It had bright red berries on it. It was rooted there in the center of the setting sun.

I stopped, stood there—awestruck at this Burning Bush. It was on fire with the passion of life. I was experiencing the Divine in a single moment that would change my life forever.

Haven't we all been surprised by God in a particular moment of life?

God, Yahweh, I AM, called me to go down out of the hills and free the Hebrews. I was being called to get out of myself—to risk—not to worry about myself—to worry about someone else—not just *my* family—but many families. I didn't know it then, but that is God's call to every human being—to leave self and live and die for others?

Isn't the test for every authentic God experience, every experience of the Holy, every true revelation, not Self, but Others—especially to reach out to help someone who is stuck? Aren't we called in an Encounter-with-God to reach out and deliver those who are "stuck," enslaved, powerless?

And with much reluctance, that's what I did. That's what happened. Basically, that's the whole story.

When I told Pharaoh he must free the Hebrews, he thought I was insane. He balked. But when sickness and plagues descended on his people, he relented and "let my people go."

When I told my people, they also thought I was insane. Yet, in spite of many fears, they followed me. Through water, through desert, through darkness, through confusion, because I promised them a Promised Land.

And of course I told them about Yahweh.

When things went wrong—and believe me, things went wrong—I would get away from everyone and spend time alone with Yahweh.

I was tired of their grumbling—and of my own. I was confused. I needed help. And whenever that happens, I run. Running away is my pattern. So I ran toward the hills, toward the mountains, toward Yahweh.

I listened, and listened again.

Most of the time all was silent; I was enveloped in a cloud of stillness.

But sometimes I heard I AM.

And then I would come down from the mountain with answers, revelations, commands, a covenant, my face glowing. And everyone knew I had been with Yahweh.

"Listen! Hear, O Israel," I would begin. But not everyone listened. In fact, soon after we escaped from Egypt, the "honeymoon ended." My people didn't want empty promises. They wanted food and water. They didn't want words to fill their ears. They wanted food to fill their bellies. They wanted instant Promised Land—an instant flow of milk and honey.

And all I could find for them was desert food: manna and quail and thank you, Yahweh,—some water.

They were disillusioned. I was disillusioned.

In a way I was a disaster as a leader. I wasn't a good speaker: I stuttered. My brother Aaron was better at that. I wasn't a military man. I was *just me*—someone called by God to set people free.

Yet, looking back, I can see why Yahweh called me. What I did have was persistence. I am the type of person who never gives up. I might run. I might hide. I might get angry. But I don't give up. Like a bulldog. Once you convince me of something, then watch out. I hang on. Once I start a puzzle, I don't stop until I have every last piece in place.

It took time, a very long time in the desert, for us to become a People. It took time to develop laws and traditions, customs and stories. It took years to pass over from old outlooks to new insights.

I suppose those of my people who stayed in Egypt eventually lost their identity. They probably mixed in and became part of the Egyptian "loaf of bread"—that mass of dough—Egypt—which had been the bread basket of the world when our ancestor Joseph was in charge.

People forget. What have you done for me lately? Wasn't it when Joseph was forgotten and new rulers took over that all our troubles began? And isn't it through our suffering and trouble that we begin to become the people we are called to become?

As the saying goes: "We jumped out of the frying pan and into the fire." We, the Israelites—a new grain of people—unleavened—took on our identity when we were formed and baked in the heat of the desert. We slowly became the People of Yahweh.

It wasn't an easy pregnancy.

Or an easy birth.

Or an easy childhood.

My people fought me all the way. Not seeing the Promised Land, they wanted to head back to Egypt. The known seemed better than the unknown.

Once when I was in the mountains listening for help from Yahweh, they were in the valley listening to themselves. Yahweh wasn't helping, so they turned elsewhere. They made their own god—formed in their image of what they thought life is about. They made a golden calf and began worshipping it. When I came down from the mountain and saw them in a drunken dance around the golden calf, I was furious. Like a parent who breaks dishes to get attention, I threw the book at them. I threw the commandments at them.

And maybe this is the way we wake up, the way we grow, the way we learn to truly live.

To *live* life.

Life is hungering and thirsting.

Life is walking with others, putting one foot ahead of the other, so we can get across the desert and reach our Promised Land, finding an oasis now and then, learning and letting go as we go along, picking ourselves up after each mistake.

Life is waking in the morning hoping to see a cloud in the sky—longing for the rain.

Life is being lost and hoping to find a Burning Bush glowing in the afternoon of our fears.

Life is the Passover: passing over from a youthful worship of gold, security, power and lust to the open willingness to listen to the true God. God is not the one I make God to be. (That's idolatry.) *God is who God is.* God is, I AM WHO I AM.

And that's where it all begins, "middles" and ends.

We're still not in the Promised Land. I don't have too many days left. And I suspect that when these people finally get there, there is not going to be too much milk and honey. They are going to have to work for it.

Thanks for listening to my story. I hope you have a better idea of how this all happened. I hope this gives you a glimpse of who I am.

And who I AM is.

Lessons for Life: The Pentateuch

Some people make it to the river; some cross it; some don't.

Moses didn't make it. He died before getting a chance to cross to the other side of the river.

His people did. Some 3,300 years ago, the Hebrew People crossed the Jordan River and entered the Promised Land

Their scriptures tell us that after spending forty years in the desert, the Hebrews finally crossed the river. You can find the story of how they got to the river in the first five books of the Bible: the Pentateuch.

The Pentateuch [from the Greek, *Pentateuchos, penta* meaning five and *teuchos,* meaning tool, vessel, book] is the first five books of the Jewish and Christian Scriptures.

Like all the books of the Bible, the Pentateuch gives us lessons for life.

One of the great lessons is to stop and sit by the river and reflect upon who we are, where we come from, what we're looking for.

Every person is baptized in promises. Every person is the hope of his or her parents. We migrate, move, work, always with the hope of providing a better life, a better home, a better neighborhood, a better land for our children.

Each person is the child of a promise.

And at times we forget the promise, forget our roots, forget our story.

Each of us needs to take time to return to the river. We need to be baptized in the stories of our parents and grandparents.

That's what the Scriptures are: a river of stories. They teach us the lessons of life—stories and examples about our sources and where we're flowing.

The Pentateuch, like all the ancient writings in the Bible, contains many, many stories, about a lot of people, and give us an abundance of lessons. Those stories connect with our stories. Other lives tell us about our lives. That's the reason we love stories.

The story of creation in Genesis is everyone's dream. We all want to make the place we raise our kids a paradise. That's the dream: a home of our own with a backyard, a garden, and trees.

Aren't the elements of the love story of Jacob and Rachel found in every love story? Every couple can resonate with the following statement in the book of Genesis; "To win Rachel, Jacob worked seven years, and they seemed to him like a few days because he loved her so much" (Genesis 29:20).

Isn't the story toward the end of Genesis about Joseph and his brothers the story of many families? Rivalry and jealousy can get us to do some destructive things to each other.

The story of Exodus is the story of every person and every group that is trapped, "stuck," sinning or sinned against. Everyone needs an exit. Everyone who is addicted needs to take steps, first step, second step, twelfth step, to move away from slavery.

In Exodus, isn't the story of the people grumbling about the desert, our story too? We want freedom. We want solutions. We want salvation. We want redemption. And don't delay, because we can't wait.

Isn't the listing of all those laws that can be found in the books of Exodus, Leviticus, Numbers and Deuteronomy, a glimpse of what every group does?

We all come up with so many rules and regulations! Red tape! Restrictions!

And at times, don't we resent rules and regulations, laws and restrictions? They inconvenience us. Tourist wisdom like: "Don't drink the water" is not enough. Rules, standards, clean air and clean water acts, how to use chemicals, how to deal with sewage, garbage, and waste disposal, are issues that need to be checked and taken care of around the world.

Take the time to read about Moses. We don't always like our leaders. We don't want someone else to be "superior." We prefer being our own boss. We like independence—that is until we have to face big issues—massive tragedies—like floods and fires, earthquakes, hurricanes, and wars. Then we want leaders and we want them to be good ones. Like Moses . . .

Moses never made it to the Promised Land.

Often parents don't see the results of their sacrifices.

There are leaders who fail to realize the results of their protests, sit-down strikes, imprisonments.

And Moses wasn't able to sit down on the other side of the Jordan to enjoy its milk and honey.

It's likely that there were many nights he knelt down in prayer and asked God, "Is it all worth it?"

We need to pray, to take time to reflect on the river of our life and when we do, we are able to see that sacrifices in life are worth it.

They are. Isn't that life's great lesson?

Life:
Turning Page After Page

'Life comes one day at a time, a page at a time, flowing on and on.

The Bible does not end when one finishes the last page of the Pentateuch. We can turn the page and begin reading what happened next, what happened when the children of Israel crossed the Jordan river.

The Book of Joshua begins the "rest of the story"—or better, the next twist and turn of Israel's history.

Beginnings and endings are often easy compared to the long mornings and afternoons of life.

As we turn the pages, as we come to rivers, we discover that our life, like a river, goes on and on—with twists and turns, slow spots and rapids, blockages and droughts, then flowing again and meeting and joining with other rivers—going on and on and on.

Read the Bible and you'll be reading your story.

The name "Joshua" or "Yehoshua" has its roots in the Hebrew word for "salvation." Joshua was a minor character in the Pentateuch, but after Moses' death, he became a main character. He became a savior.

Isn't that our story? Sometimes we're *center stage* and sometimes we're waiting in the wings wondering when it will be our turn to get out onto the stage. Will we know our lines?

We've all heard the cliché: "Hard act to follow." It's hard to follow a great person like Moses. Comparisons can kill. Sometimes people would rather follow a weak person or even a disaster. Most of the time we have no choice. It was Joshua's role to succeed Moses and he did. He goes down in Israel's history as an essential section of the river called Israel.

But Joshua didn't have to do it alone. He had Moses as his model. The God of Israel, Yahweh, was walking with him as well as with the people. This is the key theme of the Book of Joshua. It's the same message that we have in the Pentateuch and all through the Scriptures: "I AM with you."

Step by step, day by day, I AM walking with you all days, all ways, to the end of the world.

It's worthwhile to open The Book of Joshua and begin reading. Its words are worth reflecting upon.

Listen to its opening: "When Moses the servant of Yahweh had died, Yahweh spoke to Joshua. He was the son of Nun; Moses' next-in-charge. 'Moses my servant is dead. Stand up! Here is the place and now is the time to cross the Jordan. You and all the people with you are to go into the land which I am giving the children of Israel. Every place you step on with the soles of your feet, I shall give you. This is exactly what I told Moses that I would do. Your territory will go from the wilderness, to Lebanon, to the great river Euphrates, to the Great Sea westward. As long as you live, no one will be able to stand in your way. I will be with you just as I was with Moses. I will never leave you, nor desert you.'"

Now of course, all this was written down long after these events took place. And a lot of things happened. Surprise! There were people living in the Promised Land. Surprise! That makes a big difference.

Read the rest of the story—the books of the Bible from Joshua to Kings, from Isaiah the Prophet to the 12 minor prophets—and you'll find out that crossing the river into the Promised Land wasn't entering a National Park. It wasn't a place with empty picnic tables. It wasn't a place with beautiful green fields and bright flowers waiting to be cultivated and herds of cows waiting to be milked. It wasn't a picnic. It wasn't a land flowing with milk and honey.

It's like the story that Sam Levenson, the school teacher and television comedian, used to tell, "Before my parents came to America, they were told that its streets were paved with gold. Well, when they came to America, wow, were they surprised! The streets were not paved with gold. They weren't even paved. In fact, they were the ones who were expected to pave them."

Start reading the Bible from Joshua on and you'll find out that it was quite a struggle to make it a Promised Land—a land flowing with milk and honey.

Moses got the people to move toward the Promised Land. It was now up to Joshua to do things to make the promise a reality.

Like much of the story in the Pentateuch, Israel's history from Joshua onwards comes out of reflection, meditation and hindsight. It is a religious history that gives lessons to be learned. It is a history that was edited and re-edited as the nation went through its changes and its development, its ups and downs. Powerful moments and powerful people appear in its pages: the fall of Jericho; wars and rumors of wars; establishing cities; dividing up the land; Deborah; Gideon; Jephthah and his daughter; Samson; Ruth; Samuel; Saul; David; Solomon; Ahab and Jezebel; Elijah and Elisha; Isaiah; Jeremiah; the Destruction of Jerusalem by the Babylonians; the great disaster called the Exile in Babylon; Ezekiel; the return from the Exile; etc.

Specialists and commentators on the Bible have various theories about how the Bible was put together. Often it's the victor who gets to tell the story.

Common sense tells us that stories change with time. Stories get better or worse depending on who's telling the tale. We all do this. We all edit and re-edit the account of our life and our family's life.

And it's in the retelling that we often begin to really understand the story of our life.

Things Come in Threes, Don't They?

Things often come in threes.

I have discovered that coming up with three examples or three suggestions or three issues can be very helpful and lead to useful insights.

Here are some "threes" that may be thought provoking or conversation starters. Pen in hand, alone or with others, try to list the following:

The three *best* days of my life so far . . .

The three most *important* days of my life so far . . .

My three best teachers . . .

The three best weddings I've ever attended . . .

My three favorite books . . .

The three best sermons I've ever heard . . .

My three favorite movies . . .

The three best meals I've ever eaten . . .

My three favorite songs . . .

My three best vacations . . .

My three best friends . . .

Name three people I can tell everything to . . .

Name three things I don't like to discover in others . . .

My three worst mistakes . . .

Three things I love . . .

Three things I would die for . . .

The three most interesting persons I have ever met . . .

My three best memories of my father . . .

My three best memories of my mother . . .

My three earliest memories . . .

Three things I look forward to . . .

Three things I would like to be remembered for . . .

The three most important things I have ever done . . .

Three gifts I have . . .

The three persons who have had the greatest influence on my life . . .

The Three Persons Who had the Greatest Influence on My Life

$\mathcal{Y}$ears ago, the historian, H.G. Wells, was asked to name the three greatest persons in the history of the world.

His answer came in the form of an essay: "The Three Greatest Men In History." Jesus, Buddha, and Aristotle, in that order, were his three top choices.

In doing this, Wells called himself a historian, rather than a Christian. He said that Jesus, as a man, had the greatest impact on the history of the world. He also said, "The historian's test of an individual's greatness is 'What did he leave to grow? Did he start men to thinking along fresh lines with a vigor that persisted after him?' By this test Jesus stands first."

I can't name the three greatest persons in history, but I can name the three persons, I believe, had the most influence on me.

First, like Wells, I would put Jesus Christ as having the greatest influence on my life.

Being baptized a Christian, raised in a Catholic family, and having gone to Catholic schools, obviously I heard about Jesus and his teachings all through my early years.

In 1959, at the age of 20, I experienced Jesus as someone more than a historical figure. I had what is called a "religious experience." I was simply in a chapel praying and I experienced Jesus in a new way. I didn't see lightning or hear thunder. It was simply a quiet realization that Jesus knew me and loved me. That was it. To me, "Jesus is Lord!"

In the years that followed, there were many such moments in prayer, in traffic, in planes, in crowds, in cemeteries, in church, while visiting the sick, while hiking in the mountains.

Obviously Jesus' teachings in the New Testament have had a great impact. Like so many Christians, I have my favorite texts. If I had to list three, they would be:

1) "This is my body . . . This is my blood . . . which I am giving to you." (Luke 22:19-20)

2) "Forgive seventy-times-seven times." (Matthew 18:21)

3) "Go the extra mile." (Matthew 5:41)

Somewhere along the line I began to say the words "This is my body . . . This is my blood . . . " not only over the bread and the wine, but also over everyone. To me, we are all the body of Christ. And when I am with people at other times, especially babies and the very old in nursing homes, I often experience people emanating the Divine.

The second person I would name as having the greatest influence on me would be my Dad.

My father was a quiet man. His name was Michael, but everyone called him "Mike." He came to the United States in 1925. He was very quiet—an introvert, someone who liked to listen, to read poetry, to watch—and then sometime later he would make smiling and interesting observations about what he saw. He was a very good father, a hard worker, always there, always did the dishes after supper, was very neat, loved sports, loved people much more, always taking us to the park on Sundays to give my mother a break.

Recently, standing outside of church, a lady said to me, "Look at that!" pointing to a father coming out of church holding his infant daughter or son, "You never saw a father holding a baby when I was a kid." I quietly smiled. My dad always had us cradled in his arms when we were babies. You should see our family photos. He was always holding us: in the park, in the backyard, on the front stoop of our house in Brooklyn.

My Dad worked for Nabisco. He would get up early, very early, and take the subway to work. One morning I was to serve the 6:00 a.m. weekday Mass as altar boy. For some reason, that morning I was at church earlier than usual. I opened the church door on the right, walked down the side aisle, and surprise, there was my Dad kneeling in prayer. I thought he had long since gone to work. When I came out to serve mass, I glanced over to where he had been praying. He was gone. How much did that moment affect my life? What about all the other times I saw him praying the rosary or with his prayer book?

I'm still trying to figure out how much I am like my Dad. People tell me that I have his smile and his mannerisms. I walk funny, like a penguin, with my feet the opposite of being pigeon-toed. I once smiled when I saw a photo of my dad as a young man. There he was with his feet pointed out, just like me. I had never noticed that while he was living. What else didn't I notice? He died when I was thirty. I wish he had lived another twenty years, because the questions, the *real* questions I'd love to ask him, came to mind after I was thirty-five.

The third person who had the greatest influence on me would be my Mom.

My mother was quiet, but not as quiet as my Dad. She was strong, sharp, funny, prided herself as a good card player, *loved to win.* We once caught her cheating at cards. She peeked at my brother's hand when he went into the kitchen and someone else went to the bathroom. We kidded her. I think that was the only time I ever saw her angry. She was a letter-writer and loved to slip into letters twenty dollar bills wrapped in aluminum foil. She made great gravy. She loved life, work and rye bread—but it had to have cold butter on it.

My Mom was the oldest in her family. My Dad was the youngest. If there was a "boss," my Mom was the boss. After raising four kids, she went to work cleaning offices in New York City and worked her way up to shop steward. She loved making money, so she could give it away.

My Mom's Mom, age 17, came from Ireland in the late 1800s. She was living and working in Boston and loving it. Her Dad in Ireland kept asking persons from their village going to Boston to ask her to come home. She finally did in 1904 when he duped her by sending a message that he was dying. He wanted her back there in Galway to get her married and keep the family homestead going. So she married and settled in Ireland. Then it became her goal in life to get my mother to America as well as most of her other children, so that they could do the things in America that she had wanted to do.

Being the oldest, my mother, was the first to come to America. Aged 18, she landed in the United States on December 7, 1924. She loved to tell us about the days she worked as a maid in the Adams Hotel in Boston as well as for a Mrs. Brandt, who was an aunt of Charles Lindbergh. My Mom met and served Charles Lindbergh as well as Ann Morrow. She loved to tell us about the Irish dances on Friday and Saturday nights in Boston. Yet, work was the main thing. Her job was to make money and send it back to Ireland. And most of what she earned helped bring her brothers to America.

Concern for others . . . working for others . . . an eye on others . . . my Mother. How much did all of this influence me? Very, very much . . .

Jesus, Dad, and Mom: the three persons who had the greatest influence on my life, the three channels through which the great graces of my life have flowed . . .

The Earth Listens

The earth listens.

It hears alarm clocks and roosters and clock radios and spouses and people waking up every morning.

The earth listens.

It hears radio and television morning news programs telling people the latest things that have happened during the night around the world.

The earth listens.

It hears the stubborn chugging of a lazy motor in an old car, as Ruth, a 65-year-old single woman tries to get it started at 5:30 on a cold winter morning. She has to get downtown to put on the coffee, the first step in her waitress job every morning for the past 27 years at Charlie's, the local restaurant. There she will greet truck drivers, townsfolk, and friends, each with her famous smile and her raspy cigarette voice.

The earth listens.

It hears people greeting each other all around the world: "Good morning," "Buon giorno," "Guten tag," . . .

The earth listens.

It hears the cries of a newborn baby screaming the same sounds translated into every language, "Ready or not, here I come. I am here."

The earth listens.

It feels a child's first steps and parents clapping that their darling has taken this new step in life.

The earth listens.

It hears people all around the world asking about how the stock market, or a sports team, or a sick parent or child is doing.

The earth listens.

It hears the screams of the martyred as their blood seeps into its soil and covers the caskets of loved ones as everyone heads home from the cemetery not knowing how life will be after this, another death in the family.

The earth listens.

It hears the roar of the crowd at the soccer field as the home team finally scores a go-ahead goal. It hears the grunts and the groans and the breath of the players running down below on the green field.

The earth listens.

It hears music and dancing at a wedding. It feels the feet and the beat of the dancers. Sometimes it's slow dancing, and sometimes the sweat is flowing.

The earth listens.

It hears the roar of a 757 jet rolling down the runway taking 200 people off to somewhere else on the earth just seconds and yards away from another jet that is landing. And just seconds and yards away it hears people praying for safe trips after waving good bye and prayers of thanksgiving from others because of safe arrivals. It hears welcome words of love, "I missed you" as well as the lonely sound of the words, "I'll miss you."

The earth listens.

It hears the laughter and joy of card players late into a Friday night. "Thank God It's Friday."

The earth listens.

It hears a homeless addict on a metal grating mumbling, "God, it's cold out here on this cold cardboard tonight!"

The earth listens.

It hears the cries and the prayers of a mother crying for her Prodigal Daughter to come home, no questions asked, wondering where she is suffering in the night.

The earth listens.

It hears church bells, music accompanying those on their way to church on a Sunday morning, as well as those on their way to work a second job, because there are all these kids to feed and to make sure they get a good education.

The earth listens.

The earth hears the hopes of all for more—especially the poor.

The Lord hears the cries of the poor.

Do I?

Places in the Heart

"Where is your favorite place on earth and why?"

A moonlit evening on Montego Bay, Jamaica? Along the Seine River at night in Paris? Watching a sunset on a beach in Hawaii? A place where you left your heart in San Francisco? A Buddhist monastery in Kyoto, Japan? A mountain pass in the Alps? Visiting the great shrine of Mary in Lourdes, France? The beaches of Rio de Janeiro, Brazil? Driving along, no rush, in the hollows of West Virginia? Sitting with a cup of coffee on your back porch on a summer morning?

Ernest Hemingway wrote, "If you are lucky enough to have lived in Paris as a young man, then wherever you go for the rest of your life, it stays with you, for Paris is a moveable feast."

While working for a month in Canada, in the city of Saint John, New Brunswick, I noticed a weekly feature in a local newspaper magazine, entitled, "Places in the Heart." The idea was simple. The editors note stated: "Send us a photo of your favorite place and a note explaining why to Places in the Heart, *The New Brunswick Reader,* P.O. Box 2350, Saint John, N.B., E2L 3V8."

Each week I looked forward to a photo of someone's favorite place as well as their "why."

Deborah Murray sent in a picture of a rocky beach on the Restigouche River in Flatlands, New Brunswick. No people were in the picture—just rocks and river, trees and mountains. It was the place where she used to go as a child with her parents and now as an adult with her own kids. There they have spent many summers, swimming, relaxing, cooking hot dogs, and studying rocks, hoping to find images of shells and fossils that could go back millions and millions of years.

Ann Lovoie also sent in a picture of a river, the Patapedia River, New Brunswick which flows into the Restigouche. In her note she says that the spot she loves is quite secluded. "Every year I look forward to my early fall trip to this little Eden and despite the new river sounds which include the noise of logging machinery, I look forward to another spiritual experience on this river of rivers."

Carolyn Molson sent in a picture of a lone person in a canoe rowing across Belleisle Bay along the Kingston Peninsula. It's morning. It's misty. A church steeple, lots of trees, and the morning sky is in the distance. She took the picture while participating in a photography workshop—a dream she finally fulfilled. She ends her "why" with these words, "Thank you at the *Reader* for making these memories last."

Water, water, everywhere . . . People seem to love places where there is water.

Now, if you like places with lots of water, drive along the coast line of the province of New Brunswick in Canada. It has water—lots of water. See the famous Bay of Fundy, which has the highest tides in the world. Twice each day, 100 billion tons of rolling sea water funnels its way into the bay. See how the tides have sculpted huge statues, like those big statues on Easter Island, off Chile in South America. The water rises sometimes over forty-eight feet at the Bay's eastern end.

See the famous "Reversing Falls" in the City of Saint John. It's a somewhat narrow channel where the 450-mile-long St. John River empties into the Bay of Fundy. When the tide is coming in full power ahead, it pushes the river back up stream, creating a great churning of the waters, a nice postcard tourist attraction.

I didn't see much of New Brunswick during my month there, but from what I did see, they will never run out of "Places in the Heart" in that weekly newspaper magazine feature.

People love places where there is water.

And those places are everywhere. When photos of the earth are sent down from satellites we see how much of the Earth is water—covering about seventy percent of the its surface.

If you wanted to send in a photo of your favorite place, where would it be? What would be your "places in the heart"?

Would it be a scene that included water? Or mountains? Or skyscrapers?

I began to think about the many places where I've been blessed to live parts of my life:

Brooklyn, New York.

North East, Pennsylvania.

Ilchester, Maryland.

Esopus, New York.

Annapolis, Maryland.

Manhattan, NYC, New York.

West End, Long Branch, New Jersey.

Washington, District of Columbia.

Tobyhanna, Pennsylvania.

Oconomowoc, Wisconsin.

And now Lima, Ohio.

Surprise! Many of these places are near water. Lima, Ohio, where I'm living now, is far from the ocean, the Great Lakes, but it does have large earthen reservoirs. It's a delight to walk the almost four-mile path around Bresler Reservoir, especially in the cool of the evening as the sun sets.

Water: living near water . . .

My mom and dad raised us in Brooklyn, New York within sight of the Narrows—the place where the Hudson River and the East River end and then the water works its way out toward the Atlantic. I lived for six years in North East, Pennsylvania, not too far from Lake Erie. I lived for one year in Ilchester, Maryland, right next to the Patapsco River. I lived for fourteen years in Esopus, New York, right on the Hudson River. I lived for seven years in Long Branch, New Jersey, right on the edge of the Atlantic Ocean. I lived for one year on the shore of a beautiful lake in Oconomowoc Wisconsin. I lived for seven years in the Pocono Mountains, in a place called Tobyhanna—the Indian word for "ruddy waters"—a small stream not far from a large lake in a nearby State Park.

Water, water, everywhere . . . Have you been so blessed as to experience nature's beautiful water spots? Are your "places in the heart" connected with water?

I think of Herman Melville's statement about water in the first chapter of his novel, *Moby Dick*. "Yes, as everyone knows, meditation and water are wedded forever... Why did the old Persians hold the sea holy? Why did the Greeks give it a separate deity . . . ? Surely all this is not without meaning. And still deeper the meaning of that story of Narcissus, who because he could not grasp the tormenting, mild image he saw in the fountain, plunged into it and was drowned. But that same image, we ourselves see in all rivers and oceans. It is the image of the ungraspable phantom of life; and this is the key to it all."

I think of the various ways the prophets told people to "come to the waters" to be washed and restored and renewed.

John the Baptist calling people to the Jordan River to be baptized and to start again . . .

Jesus going to the Jordan, as well as the Sea of Galilee, in a land that features sand and heat, more than water and coolness.

I think of the first time I saw the spot in Ireland where my Mom and Dad were born. Both their homes were right on the edge of Galway Bay, looking out at the Aran Islands, looking out into the Atlantic.

What would be my *favorite* "place in the heart"?

My choice—after much reflection—would be a beautiful mountain lake, high up the Rockies. One summer, I was backpacking with friends in Colorado and some people who met us on a path told us about this magnificent place to see. We followed their directions and climbed up a steep path. There it was—an enclave in the rocks—a natural cathedral, no roof, but it held a small lake where a sanctuary would be. Looking at our maps we learned its name: "Lake of Solitude."

Standing there, awestruck by the beauty before us, we spontaneously said the Lord's Prayer out loud. Then we took pictures.

All these years I've never needed those photos to remind me of that place. I can simply close my eyes, picture it, and be there. I suppose time and memory and the people we are with are the ingredients that create "places in the heart."

Mr. P

"Oh, I have feelings. That's not the problem. Everyone has feelings, right?"

"Right."

"The problem is knowing . . . knowing what you're feeling . . . knowing what you're going through . . . knowing what you're doing."

"Knowing?"

"Yeah, knowing. Okay, 'knowing' might not be the right word. But something like that. Knowing, understanding, realizing, being sure just what's going on inside of me. That's what I'm trying to see and to tell you about."

"Okay."

"You know, feelings are invisible. They're not 'apples or oranges,' as the cliché goes. They're there, but you can't open up a person like a refrigerator and take out a feeling and put it on the table and look at it."

"Right."

"Well, there are feelings in here—sometimes here in my chest and sometimes here in my mind—and sometimes they're bouncing like crazy around inside of me. I can feel them all over my body. Does that make any sense?"

"Yes."

"I guess people are like a lake or an ocean. Yeah, an ocean. Sometimes we're calm. All we see is the surface and tiny waves. But sometimes we're all waves, crashing and smashing against the shore. And when I'm in a storm, people stay clear of me.

"Now, that doesn't happen too often. Usually, I'm a pretty low-key person."

"I agree. That's a good description of you."

"Yeah, I'm like an ocean—calm on the surface, but lots of things underneath. An ocean, yeah, I like that. I am an ocean. I never thought of that. That's good. An ocean. Thanks for listening to me. Really. Very few people have ever taken the time to listen to me. I think I scare people off with my silence and my feelings. But I think everyone gets nervous when the other person is feeling their feelings, especially loud feelings."

"Yeah, I agree. I know I get nervous with other people's feelings."

"You do? Okay, then you understand."

"Well, a little bit, but keep talking."

"Well, let's get back to the ocean. I like that image. I'll have to think about that a lot more. An ocean. I like the ocean. In fact, that wouldn't be a bad nickname to have, 'Ocean.'"

"Nickname?"

"Yeah, nickname. Nobody every calls me by my first name. I'm always a nickname."

"What do you mean?"

"Well, when I was a kid, they always called me 'Porky' and I always hated it."

"Why 'Porky'? That sounds so cruel."

"You mean that?"

"Yeah."

"Well, when I was a kid, I was short and stocky and the kids would 'Oink, oink,' at me all the time."

"Oooh!"

"Yeah, and being kids, nobody ever stopped to realize that kids can be cruel to each other."

"Right!"

"And to be honest, I have to admit that I was cruel to other kids, especially to those who were cruel to me."

"Yeah."

"And then I'd get home and nobody in our house would have any time for me. I understand it now, but back then when I was a kid, that hurt. We were a big family. Sometimes I would be hurting. Sometimes I'd be happy. Like everyone else, I had feelings. But back then, I didn't know about feelings. Hey, I was a just a kid. I'd be happy or angry or cranky or sleepy or high energy—all depending on what I could see, or what was going on, or what day it was."

"Day?"

"Yeah, day. I remember that I always loved Saturdays, especially Saturday mornings. I could just sleep or get up any time I wanted. It all depended on what was happening. On Saturday's I could just blend into the woodwork. Nobody was on anybody's case on Saturday morning in our house. And most Saturday mornings we could eat what we wanted or watch TV or play ball or whatever.

"Oh."

"But schooldays and some Sundays, there would be a fight at home or in school over nicknames or about sharing toys or eating vegetables or bumping someone too hard. And then there would be lots of feelings and lots of repercussions."

"Oh."

"And when I was older, like married, she said I never expressed my feelings. She said all I ever could do was 'grunt', that I was stunted and stupid."

"Oooh!"

"We went for marriage counseling and all that. Both of them—the therapist and my wife—kept hitting me with the word 'feelings.' Feelings, feelings, feelings: they rubbed feelings in my face. I still didn't have a clue about what feelings were. I felt like crying. I felt like walking out. I felt so empty in the center of my chest."

"Oh!"

"But it was she who walked out."

"Oh?"

"Yeah, she just upped and walked out on me. And so I was all alone again, just like when I was a kid. When I was a kid they picked on me for being slow. I was a B student most of the time. And most of the time, I just existed. I was growing up. Maybe my parents didn't have enough energy. Looking back now I can understand that. I had an older brother and two older sisters and a younger brother. I was lost there almost at the bottom of our family. So I kept moving, existing, I guess, just doing what kids do."

"Oh."

"But looking back now I think I simply blended, hiding right there near the bottom, building a shell, a hard shell to protect myself. Look at my back. I've always been slumped over a bit. I think this was one of the reasons why the other kids called me 'Porky.' When they saw me, they would go 'oink, oink.'"

"Oh."

"Maybe they were right. I was a grunter."

"Oh."

"Then in my teenage years, to protect myself from kids my age, I needed more and more protection. Teenagers can be tough. I had bad acne and anxiety and sexual feelings and all that stuff teenagers go through. I had few clues on what was happening—but not enough. So at some point in the middle of all that I changed. I think for the worse. I attacked back. When attacked, I attacked. If I was shot at with digs, I'd shoot back with cracks and comments. I dressed tougher too. Then came the cruelest nickname: 'Porcupine.' I switched from being called 'Porky' to 'Porcupine.'"

"They called you 'Porcupine'?"

"Yeah, that was my nickname from twelve to twenty. And they were right. Nobody could get near me. Well, eventually someone did, my wife. I guess she saw me as a project. She always said that I was just like her father. Stupid me, didn't get it. She was going to change me to be what she wanted her father to be. Like me, he never said anything. Kept everything in. So I guess she felt sorry for me. She was going to save me. She was going to change me from being a 'Porcupine' into a human being. Now of course, neither of us knew this was going on, so we got married."

"Oh."

"Well, it didn't work. I didn't change. We tried to have kids. We didn't. I've often wondered if kids would have changed me. I do a lot of wondering. Would kids have saved our marriage? Heck, would kids have saved me? I often wondered if kids would have warmed me up. I don't know. I guess that was her plan too. But having kids didn't change her father."

"Oh."

"I've often wondered what would have happened if kids started swimming in this ocean called me. I don't know."

"Good question."

"Wait, let me tell you one last thing. At work, when I became a manager, I ended up with a new nickname. Everyone called me 'Mr. P.' At first it didn't bother me. It was better than being called 'Porky' or 'Porcupine.' But then, it started to bother me—bother me big time. It was just another damn nickname. I just wish somewhere along the line, someone would stop and look me in the eye and see me as me. Me. Me. Alive. Me. Here. A person. Someone with feelings—deep feelings—as deep as the ocean."

"Wooooo! That's tough stuff, Pete. I never heard you talk like this before. Listen. I was about to get going, but let's order another beer and continue this conversation. You triggered something in me that I've never told anybody about before . . . "

"Oh."

Complimenting God

*P*rayer is contemplating God.

Prayer is also complementing God.

Prayer is contemplating and complimenting . . . Looking around and seeing that everything leads to love . . .

Prayer is being mindful of who I am, who you are, and who God is, and this leads to a sense of awe, a sense of wonder . . .

Prayer is walking this earth with an attitude of gratitude . . .

Prayer is stopping to notice and thanking God for our daily bread . . .

Gratitude makes us graceful.

Prayer is taking time out to thank God for the gift of life, for being here, being able to describe who we are with God's words, "I Am Who I Am;" being able to meet and greet God each morning by saying, "Here I am, God. I want to thank You for the gift of life, being on Your earth this day with all my sisters and brothers. Thank you! Help me to make this a good day for everyone I meet. Amen."

Prayer is a noticing that leads to songs and echoes, words and silence, awe and service flowing out of our center into our Center: God.

Read the Psalms.

Read the hymns in our hymnbooks.

Read other people's prayers.

Ask others whether they pray. If they say, "Yes," then ask them about God. Sort of interview them. Listen to them. Hear their story.

Discover people of prayer. Let them take you into their Center. Ask them good questions and listen for their answers.

Discover people of service. Let them take you into their Center. Ask them good questions and then listen for their answers.

Look carefully at the word "religion". See "lig" in the middle of the word? "Ligare" is the Latin word to tie or to bind. "Ligamentum" means what the word sounds like in English, "ligaments"—those cords that athletes rip when they're injured. They tie us together inside.

Religion is what binds us together inside, what connects us, what we wrap our life around.

Be careful. If you buy that definition of religion, you're "caught."

Accept that definition of religion and you have to admit everyone has a religion.

With that settled, the only question left is, "What is your religion?"

And then the conversation—the great conversation on the meaning of life—can really begin.

Everyone has a religion—because everyone has a center—and in that center you'll discover people's belief systems. Those who are trying to shut down other people's religious practices are doing it because of their own religious beliefs and practices.

There is no way out of this dilemma except conversation and conversion (meaning change) compromise and working together instead of fighting each other.

Prayer is understanding this.

Awe-filled moments and awful moments call forth response from our belief systems, from our Center, from our very being.

Whom do we credit for the cry and the beauty of a newborn baby? Whom do we blame for the stillborn baby? Whom do we credit for the beauty of a mountain meadow? Whom do we blame for an earthquake or a plane crash or a polluted river?

Religions—Religions with a capital "R"—give some answers to these questions.

Everyone reacts and responds to the good, the bad and the ugly.

Picture someone going to an art museum. They walk around looking at the paintings and the sculptures. They praise some painter or sculptor for a work of art that evokes from their center a "Wow!" or they laugh or complain about some work of art that evokes a feeling of "Awful!"

Next picture that person leaving the museum. They walk down the front steps and they suddenly stop. They stop to contemplate a Japanese maple tree planted right in the center of the front lawn of the art museum. "Wow!" It's a moment of awe.

The museum worked. They didn't notice the tree on the way in, but they notice it on the way out. Then they continue down the rest of the steps to the street in front of the museum. They stop again. "Parked" right there in front of the museum they see an abandoned car, It's beat up. Its tires, windows, and doors are missing. Out loud for all to hear, they yell, "Awful. What a disgrace! Why doesn't someone tow this mess away?" They didn't notice the car on the way in.

The museum "worked."

Judaism, Christianity, Islam, and other religions of the world claim that God is the Creator of all of us and this Earth we walk upon.

Prayer is a seeing, a listening, a contemplation, that flows into "praise" and "thanks" to God for all these creations.

What about the ugly? What about the "mistakes"? What about envy and earthquakes?

Judaism, Christianity, Islam, and other religions of the world give various answers to these questions. Sometimes the answers lead to praise, but most of the time they lead us to believe and trust in God.

I've heard people say that God has no need for our praise. God is God. And I've heard people say, "But we need to hear ourselves praising God." But it's more than that.

Does God need compliments?

I don't know. God is Dark Mystery!

I don't know whether God wants or needs compliments, and to be honest, down deep I think it doesn't matter. All I know is that I want to thank God for all that is, for the gift of life, for all I see and all I have received and for every person on the planet.

If you're not sure there is a God, go to Zion National Park in southern Utah and come back and tell me you stood there and didn't compliment God.

We all have a creed.

Listen to yourself, and you'll find yourself saying "I believe" surprisingly often.

I believe everyone, down deep, has a faith in God. Why? Because the principle of cause and effect is so built into human beings that we have to believe that Someone caused the universe.

Cause and effect is a ligament in our soul.

If I look into the night sky, if I look at Lake Michigan, or the turquoise waters of the Caribbean, and have feelings of awe, then I can sense that someone designed, shaped, arranged and created all I see.

I call that Someone "God" and I'm working on giving God compliments.

No, No, Nanette

*I*t was a Wednesday matinee on Broadway.

As we edged our way to our places, I realized that these were not going to be great seats. I wasn't paying, so I didn't complain.

I was with twelve people, mostly women, our Retreat House staff from New Jersey. Once a year we would try to catch a Broadway Play and go to a dinner in New York City. This year it was a revival of an old favorite, *No, No, Nanette.*

"No, No," I hadn't seen the original. (Before my time.)

We were early, so I scanned the audience. It was made up mostly of older people, women, and probably retirees. The rest of the world was out in the "real world," working, or in school.

Our seats were near the upper right wall looking directly down, not onto the stage, but into the orchestra pit. The curtain wasn't open yet, but I could already figure out that we'd be able to see only the left side wall of the set, and the first thirty feet of the stage. We could hope, most of the action would be in the front of the stage and to the left. Well, at least we'd get the lines, and I was in good company.

It was to be a fine musical—lots of laughs, good singers and dancers, good actors. It was to be a joyful day: excellent theater, followed by a delicious dinner, a staff doing something together besides work.

Little did I know when the afternoon began that what I would remember for all these years was what took place, not on the stage, but directly down below us in the orchestra pit.

Before the play started, the orchestra members appeared and took their seats. I could see everything they did; from the opening of violin cases to the putting of a handkerchief in a handy place on a music stand. I watched the "Hi's" to someone coming in at the last minute. I watched the musicians setting up their music and adjusting their strings.

I had seen musicals and plays before, but I'd never seen an orchestra pit from above.

Then I noticed it: one of the violinists took out a copy of the *Daily News* and put it on his music stand. The curtains opened and the play began. The violinist proceeded to read the newspaper from front to back through the play!

Apparently, he had all the songs perfectly memorized and didn't miss a note—or a beat.

Shakespeare said in *Hamlet* that the purpose of the play is "To hold, as 'twere, the mirror up to nature . . ."

I saw myself there in the orchestra pit. A mirror was held up to me that day. That musician was doing something I've been doing all my life: in classrooms, in conversations, in church, I've played the music, but I've been doing something else. My attention, my mind, my heart, my very being has so many times been somewhere else "a million miles away."

"No, No, . . ."

Hitting Thirty

When does a person really begin to see?

Is it after their first major failure, their first "real love," their first child, a war, a crash, their first experience of having someone they love die?

How old were Adam and Eve when they had to leave the garden? How old was Judas when he betrayed Jesus?

Think about the Buddha. He was about twenty-nine when he was "enlightened." He experienced what are called in Buddhism, the Four Signs or the Four Sights: a dead body, a sick person, an old person, and a wandering monk with a beggar's bowl.

What did he learn when he observed these four sights?

He saw that something was missing in his life. He saw that he was going to get old some day. He saw sickness, aging, and death in everyone's future. He also saw a man of peace, a holy ascetic, even though he was living on nothing but the food he received from begging.

Jesus didn't start his ministry till he was around thirty. Some say that the first big key enlightenment moment of his life came when he was being baptized in the Jordan River. He heard God, his Father, our Father, say, "You are my beloved son."

It was the great experience of being loved—being loved by God. Then for three years, for the rest of his life, Jesus went about telling everyone this same good news from God: "You are my beloved son. You are my beloved daughter."

Great experiences can't be hid under bushel baskets. They need to be shared. Once I experience being loved by God, I want everyone else to have the same experience. If I don't, then I didn't experience what Jesus experienced.

I am "Beloved" by God. God calls each of us by that name, "Beloved!"

What a great vision. What a way to see people! What a way to treat people! I'm beloved. You're beloved. By God. By me.

Have I had an "enlightenment" yet? Like that of Jesus? Like that of the Buddha?

Thirty seems to be a key age.

Is that why they had that saying in the 1960s, "Don't trust anyone over thirty?"

How old am I? Have I awakened yet? Have the illusions I had when I was young fizzled out yet—illusions about God, about my life, my future, other people, especially those over thirty?

Is thirty too young?

William James, the famous American psychologist who lived during the early part of the twentieth century said in so many words that the "crash" that wakes us up happens to two-thirds of the human race somewhere about or after thirty-five.

Carl Jung, the famous Swiss psychoanalyst, is often quoted as saying that he never succeeded in bringing a person over thirty-five to psychological health, without first facing the question of meaning, or without restoring his or her religious outlook.

In the baseball movie, *The Natural*, actress Glenn Close played the part of Iris Lemon, the woman in white, the savior figure for Robert Redford

(Roy Hobbs). The movie is based on Bernard Malamud's novel of the same name.

A key scene for me takes place when Roy and Iris talk about suffering. In the movie it happens in the hospital before the big game; in the novel it takes place at a lake.

The dialogue from the novel goes like this:

> *"I won't ever hurt you, Roy."*
>
> *"No."*
>
> *"Don't ever hurt me."*
>
> *"No."*
>
> *"What beats me," he said with a trembling voice, "is why did it always have to happen to me? Why did I deserve it?"*
>
> *"Being stopped before you started?"*
>
> *He nodded.*
>
> *"Perhaps it was because you were a good person?"*
>
> *"How's that?"*
>
> *"Experience makes good people better."*
>
> *She was staring at the lake.*
>
> *"How does it do that?"*
>
> *"Through the suffering."*
>
> *"I had enough of that," he said in disgust.*
>
> *"We have two lives, Roy, the life we learn with and the life we live with after that. Suffering is what brings us toward happiness."*
>
> *"I had it up to here." He ran a finger across his windpipe.*
>
> *"Had what?"*
>
> *"What I suffered—and I don't want any more."*

"It teaches us to want the right things."

"All it taught me is to stay away from it. I am sick of all I have suffered."

She shrank away a little.

He shut his eyes.

Afterwards, sighing, she began to rub his brow, and then his lips.

"And is that the mystery about you, Roy?"

"What mystery?"

"I don't know. Everyone seems to think there is one."

"I told you everything."

"Then there really isn't?"

"Nope."

Her cool fingers touched his eyelids. It was unaccountably sweet to him.

"You broke my jinx," he muttered.

"I'm thirty-three," she said, looking at the moonlit water.

He whistled but said, "I am no spring chicken either, honey."

Suffering . . . the cross . . . falling on our face . . . failure . . . a death . . . a divorce . . . a dumb mistake . . . a fire . . . being fired . . . betraying another . . . being betrayed . . . breaking vows . . . cancer . . . a crash . . .

Outlook . . . viewpoint . . . vision . . . seeing . . . knowing . . . waking up . . . enlightenment . . . how do I see life?

One of my favorite "see-ers" is John Dunne. He's a writer, a pilgrim, a priest, a professor of theology at Notre Dame University in Indiana. I've met him through his books. Each book provides a great deal to see.

He often says that journeys "into the different" help us to see the ordinary differently.

Prayer and meditation get us out of ourselves, urge us to make an exodus from our flesh pots, to take the exit ramp off our highway into a rest area. Prayer stops the world for a moment, takes us into the desert of our emptiness, helps us leave the crowd and take a narrow path into the mountains of our being—at times bringing us to Transfiguration, into ecstasy, bliss.

If you like to escape to quiet places to read, try John Dunne's books: *The Way of All the Earth, The City of the Gods, The Homing Spirit, The Reasons of the Heart, The House of Wisdom, Time and Myth.*

He's over thirty.

Meeting Myself

Can we meet someone we never met?

One of my favorite books is, *If You Meet The Buddha On The Road, Kill Him*. The author, Sheldon Kopp, teaches, "The most important thing that everyone must learn is that no one else can teach us."

That's a subtle statement. It's a "What?" It's like the general statement: "Never make general statements."

Obviously, others can teach us. Less obvious is the truth that good teachers help us to realize: discovering and understanding the "why" of a truth is better than memorizing a truth.

Memorizing answers might get us an "A" on a test; discovering a truth can give us "help" for life.

It's like the teaching: "If I give you a fish, you eat tonight, but if I teach you how to fish, you can eat for the rest of your life."

I remember a teacher saying as he handed out a stack of typed notes, "If these stay my notes, they'll go into your wastepaper basket or your bottom drawer, but if they become your ideas, they go into your life."

Too often education is "hand-outs", memorization, Xeroxing pieces of paper that "went" through a machine and never into a mind. Some students think that underlining or highlighting sentences in a book is studying.

People can know teachings of the Buddha or Jesus, chapter and verse, without meeting and getting to know the Buddha or Jesus or themselves.

A teacher that I had for Sacred Scripture said, "We're not going to take every book and every text of the New Testament—only a few. What I like to teach is method. The little we take, we'll take in depth. If you get the method, the process, you got the rest of your life to get the rest of the scriptures."

I was angry with that approach. "I could have killed him." It made me nervous that we weren't going to cover every chapter and verse. In time I learned, "It's the only way to go."

I sense that those who stood there in market places or on grassy hills and listened to Jesus or the Buddha speak, began to meet themselves. And I suspect that when listeners compared what was being taught to what they were living, the reaction was anger, defensiveness and a desire to assassinate the teacher.

I think that is what Sheldon Kopp is getting at when he said, *If You Meet The Buddha On The Road, Kill Him.*

Kopp is not only an author, but also a psychotherapist and a teacher. I'm sure he learned over and over again in the classroom, in therapy and in his own heart, that all of us are lazy, struggling human beings.

As I read his books, I met myself over and over again. I think that's what makes a great teacher—and a great therapist.

Like parents and teachers, therapists give answers. Yet they really can't give answers. Better: they can listen when we meet ourselves and point out landmarks in our journey.

Meeting the Buddha

As already stated, H.G. Wells thought that the Buddha was one of the three greatest people in history.

Isn't that a good reason to make the journey to meet the Buddha?

I have met the Buddha in the written word. He certainly passes the test of being a great teacher: someone "you want to kill at times". His challenges are as wrenching as those of Jesus. Buddha's teaching of eliminating desires from one's life is as tough as Jesus' words to "Turn the other cheek", "Forgive seventy times seven times", and "Lay down your life for your friends."

What did the Buddha teach about life that I can spread on the bread of my being?

Which Buddha?

The word "Buddha" is from the ancient Hindu Sanskrit and Pali word for enlightenment, *"bodhi."* Buddha simply means, "The Enlightened One" or "The Awakened One." There have been many Buddhas because there have been many "enlightened ones". The great historical Buddha was born Siddhartha Gautama some 560 years before Jesus in present-day Nepal in the foothills of the Himalayas.

Siddhartha was his first name. Gautama his family name. He is now known in history as Gautama Buddha.

When I began studying Buddhism, he is the one I've heard the most about. The story of his life, like many a famous person, contains layer upon layer of legend. Basically, his life goes like this. He is born rich. His father, like many a father, tried to shield him from life's miseries. Then when he was twenty-nine, he saw "the Four Sights:" the dead body, the sick person, the old person and the wandering monk with the beggar's bowl.

He met himself. He was looking at four possible mirrors. Till then, his father had tried to shelter him from such scenes and realities.

Shocked, he left home. He left his wife, his child, his riches, and walked around as a wandering monk in search of answers.

Doing this for a few years, he still knew that something was missing from his life.

He sat down under a fig tree and told himself that he would sit there until he understood the reason for suffering. After forty-nine days, after temptations from Mara (the Wicked One), he saw the Light. He achieved enlightenment, nirvana.

For the rest of his life he preached to others about what he saw.

What did he see? What did he teach?

Some would say that Siddhartha Gautama, the Enlightened one, the Buddha, taught nothing. You, yourself, have to see everything. You, yourself, have to meditate. You, yourself, have to learn about everything and nothing. How? By seeing? How? By sitting under your own tree, closing your eyes and then interpret what you see.

As I "sit under my tree" what do I see?

I see that I am alive, have roots, grow, and produce fruit. Then Autumn comes and leaves fall to the ground, roll and rush across the earth, till they get caught in the hedges and then decay in their final resting place.

What else do I see?

I walk down the street and see abandoned cars and empty plastic bags blowing in the wind. I pass little children filled with life, jumping rope with each other, while their grandmothers sit close by watching and knitting, talking and listening, sitting there on their light aluminum chairs. I see new skin and wrinkled skin.

What more do I see?

I observe people. Watch television. Pass time. Walk around the mall. Listen to old people. Listen to kids. I listen to others. I see that everyone is filled with expectations.

I see that advertisements aim at our desire to acquire.

We are all saying what Jesus said on the cross, "I thirst."

I see that expectations, hunger and thirst, wanting things, wears me out. Desiring what isn't, destroys me. Needing the day and night to go *my way* defeats me every day in every way.

I learned from the Buddha that the big issue is DESIRE!

I learned from the Buddha that the big problem is wanting to CONTROL.

I learned from the Buddha that the big solution is LETTING GO.

The Buddha learned that desires, cravings, hungers, thirsts, needs, lusts, "my will be done," my trying to be in control, are all the stuff of disaster. When I don't get what I want, it hurts. Not being able to accept "whatever" is the cause of our troubles. Suffering is the result of desire. Expectations can kill us.

Jesus was right: "Not *my* will be done, but *Your* will be done."

Would the Buddha then add, "Let God" as in, "Let go, let God"?

I don't know about the Buddha and God. When I study Buddhism, I read that he was an atheist or non-theist.

And to complicate things, some of his followers ended up worshipping *him* as a God.

So for some, Buddhism is a religion; for others a philosophy.

What did the Buddha teach?

Outsiders looking at the insides of Buddhism soon discover the famous "Four Noble Truths:"

1) Suffering comes with existing;

2) Suffering is caused by selfish desires;

3) Healing comes when you eliminate desire;

4) To eliminate desire, take the middle path, the "Eightfold Path," between sensuality and asceticism.

Siddhartha had learned from his experience that extremes are not the way to go. Choose the Middle Path. Avoid extremes. Beware of extreme self-indulgence and extreme self-denial.

The Middle Path has 8 steps:

right knowledge,

right intention,

right speech,

right conduct,

right means of livelihood,

right effort,

right mindfulness and

right concentration.

What else? What next?

I think that's enough for starters.

Looking at the life and teachings of Siddhartha Gautama and Buddhism, one discovers volumes—a lifetime of words.

More is sometimes better; sometimes worse. Avoid extremes.

Sit under a tree and be mindful of what is really necessary.

Look for the light.

Isn't that what we really desire?

Under a Tree

I once spent a weekend at a retreat center overlooking the Hudson River in Riverdale, New York, listening to Thomas Berry give "A New Creation Account."

A priest friend of mine, who knew me quite well, said that I would only understand about 5 percent. He was right. The ideas, the broad areas that Thomas Berry covered, were way over my head. I knew very little about anthropology and astrophysics, paleontology and paleoclimatology, geology and other "ologies." I hadn't done enough reading and looking into the writings of Mircea Eliade and Teilhard de Chardin. I didn't know the ins and outs of Buddhism, Hinduism, Confucianism and other "isms." I wasn't aware enough of the life and culture of the Native Peoples of the Americas as well as others who have walked our earth. I sat there amazed listening to hundreds of topics Thomas Berry brought into "A New Creation Account"—his telling the story, his attempt to give us an autobiography of the earth and of creation

Looking back now, years later, I'm glad I was there that weekend. It's good to sit at the feet of a great teacher and great mind—even if very little is understood. I took notes. It was good to have a list and a gist of things I needed to look at as I moved into the future.

There is one thing I remember that he said. He said it clearly and sincerely. He began his three-day creation account by saying there was a very old oak tree down near the river. He said it was estimated to be some 400 years old. He pointed toward its direction out the glass doors. We all looked out the glass doors toward the green lawn, toward the river. Thomas Berry said: "Maybe the best thing for us to do this weekend would be to go down to the river, sit under the oak tree, and watch the river flow by. I think we might get a lot more out of that than from sitting up here listening to someone talking."

Why do I remember that comment? Why did I go down to the oak tree a few times during the weekend and sit under it quietly and watch the river flow by?

I didn't know then, but I know now?

Someone said, "Don't write in your diary what happened today because you won't understand what happened till next week or next year."

There's something about sitting under a tree . . .

When we were kids, my dad used to take us every Sunday to a place called "Bliss Park." It was paradise for a kid. It was perfect for kites in November and sleigh riding in January. It had everything: hills for rolling down, a wading pool, basketball courts, a macadam softball field, seesaws, swings, slides, a beautiful view of New York Harbor, and lots of trees to sit under, especially those on top of the big hill.

I have fond memories of many Sunday afternoons running and rolling on green grass, laughing then sitting under a tree for a picnic with Mom and Dad, my two sisters and my brother. And I can still picture my Dad smiling his great smile watching us loving life in Bliss Park, while he sat there smoking his pipe.

Sitting under a tree, Siddhartha Gautama, the Buddha, meditated—vowing to remain there till he got an answer to the "why" of suffering. Finally, after forty-nine-days he was awakened, enlightened.

There's an Old Testament story about Elisha the Prophet sitting under a tree. He spoke out against King Ahab and his wife, Jezebel. The result was he had to flee. After a day's journey into the wilderness, he ran out of energy. He lay down under a small tree for rest. He began telling God to take his life. Then he fell asleep exhausted. An angel woke him and told him to "Get up and eat." The Lord fed him, and he was able to make the forty day's journey to Horeb, the mountain of God.

In the Gospel of John a man named Nathaniel was sitting under a fig tree; the next day, he met Jesus, who said that he saw him sitting under a fig tree. Something happened there. We don't know what. But Nathaniel left everything to follow Jesus.

Judas stood under a tree filled with grief because he had just betrayed his best friend. He was so miserable that he couldn't remember any of Jesus' many words about forgiveness. So he hanged himself.

Mary, the mother of Jesus, Mary's sister, Mary Magdalene, and the disciple named John, stood under the tree of the cross and heard Jesus' last words of love before he died.

The great Saint Augustine was sitting under a fig tree when his life changed and he was converted.

As school kids, we all heard the legend about Isaac Newton and how he discovered the Law of Gravity while sitting under an apple tree. An apple fell and hit him on the head, and with his great imagination he figured out the Law of Gravity. This mathematical and scientific genius wrote millions of words on all kinds of subjects, having looked into a lot more things than gravity, but for unscientific people like me, I remember only the story of the apple falling from the tree.

There's something about sitting under a tree . . .

A couple celebrating fifty years of marriage went back to their hometown for their Golden Anniversary, to the place where they began. They had a wonderful celebration with their children, grandchildren, great-grandchildren and friends.

The next day was warm and sunny. They decided to go by themselves to a nearby park—a place of memories from their greener days. Holding hands they walked along the edge of the green grass on a cement path that wasn't there when they were young. They were looking for something. They stopped. There it was, still there—their favorite tree. Now arm in arm, they danced over to it. They laughed and cried and hugged each other. Kids on the path on bikes and skateboards flew by and one almost crashed, not believing what he was seeing. They missed that. The only thing they could see was themselves, fifty years earlier, in this same spot, a young couple, in love, under this very tree, holding onto each other for life.

While sitting under a tree, did Samuel Taylor Coleridge write these words, "Flowers are lovely; love is flower like; / Friendship is a sheltering tree."?

We may sit under a tree, feeling stupid because there are so many things we don't know, from astrophysics to zoology. But as we look up at the tree, we smile. Everyone knows, young or old, smart or not, there are things we learn while sitting under a tree, that we might not learn anywhere else on earth . . .

Off On

What am I off on?

Judy is on vacation for three weeks. She comes home and there is a new boss at work and a new pastor at church. She asks her friends a simple question about each, "What is he off on?"

Is everyone off on something?

Is religion what we're off on?

Is one's religion simply what gives meaning and energy and light?

Where do I spend my time? Where do I spend my life? What am I looking for? What am I worried about? What am I trying to control? What makes me tick?

An alcoholic said, "I was looking for God at the bottom of a bottle."

Is everyone thirsty?

Is everyone searching?

Is every person in the dark, until they see the Light?

We vote with our time. We vote with our feet. We vote with where we really want to be. We vote on what we're off on? When we stop looking at our watch, it often means we're home.

Where do we feel at home? What quenches our hunger and our thirst for meaning? What gives us delight? What gives us The Light?

Haven't we all heard someone describe someone else:

"His religion is Sports."

"My daughter is wasting her life hanging around the Mall."

"He's never home. He's married to his job."

"His god is his belly."

"She's lost in lust."

"She's too wrapped up in her kids."

"I don't see my husband anymore. He spends hour after hour on his computer, late into the night."

What am I off on?

Neatness? Control? Time? Looks? Books? Work? The stock market? Money? Gadgets? Exercise? News? God? Sports?

What's my religion?

What am I off on?

Why that?

If I answer with something other than work or sports or clothes or food or exercise or looks, is it an Established Religion?

Why that Religion?

In the 1500's, in what is now Germany, when there were wars between Lutherans and Catholics, one of the principles the German princes pushed was: *"Cuius regio, eius religio."* This Latin statement is translated: "Your region, your religion." or "The region you belong to determines the religion you belong to."

It worked and it didn't work. In general, in Germany, to this day, you're more apt to find Lutherans in the north and Catholics in the south.

My parents and their parents, and their parents and their grandparents were Catholics because they lived in a Catholic region in Ireland. I am a Catholic because my parents were Catholic.

If I had been born in India, I might be a Buddhist or a Hindu or Christian. If I had been born in the Middle East I might be a Moslem, a Jew, or a Christian. If I had been born in Norway, I might be Protestant.

I was born a Christian. My Mom and Dad had me baptized as an infant, brought me to church and had me educated in a Catholic school. I heard about Jesus from my beginnings and as I grew up.

This pattern is the pattern of millions and millions of people who are called Catholics.

If we widen the dimensions to include Baptists, Lutherans, Methodists, Presbyterians, Orthodox, and many other branches of Christianity, we'll add millions and millions and millions and millions more who are called Christians.

Obviously, some born Christians are Christians in name only.

At some point, a Christian by birth has to choose as a adult, what she or he thinks about Jesus Christ.

Am I off on Jesus Christ or not?

This choice can be quite dramatic or a sort of unconscious drifting this way or that.

If I am a Christian, have I made a choice yet? If I have, was it electric and dramatic or was it slow, calm and quiet?

What's my religious story?

Christians know the story of the conversion of a man named Saul. It's told in the Christian scriptures.

Saul was off on persecuting Christians. They made his blood bubble. His goal was to rid the earth of them—well, at least to put a stop to those in his area of the world. They were going to be the ruination of his religion: Judaism. Now being a Jew didn't necessarily mean that one hated and persecuted Christians. But Saul did.

There he was on the road to a city called Damascus. It's the capital of Syria—population today around 1,250,000. Suddenly, Saul was sort of hit by lighting. He fell to the ground. He heard a voice. He was challenged to make a decision about what he was off on in his life.

The voice he heard said, "Saul, Saul, why are you persecuting me?"

Saul said, "Who are you?"

The voice answered, "I am Jesus and you are persecuting me."

Saul was stunned by the light. He saw The Light.

And then for the next thirty years, Paul was off on Jesus. He went around his world visiting Christians and proclaiming Jesus Christ to those who had not yet heard about him.

He told them about The Light that he saw and that Jesus was that Light.

Paul, who was off on persecuting Christians, was now off on proclaiming Christ to the world.

Am I still in the dark, gaining momentum, so that one of these days, I'll have a "Damascus experience"? Or will my conversion be slow—slowly realizing what I'm really off on in life?

What *am* I off on?

Christology:
Low, High or Other?

$\mathcal{H}$.G. Wells, as already stated, chose Jesus, the Buddha and Aristotle as the three most influential people in history.

What do I think about Jesus? Who do I say he is?

When Jesus of Nazareth was walking around Israel gathering, preaching, healing, and feeding those who were hungry and hurting, people asked each other, "What do you think about this Jesus."

That question pops up over and over in the four Gospels, the accounts about Jesus by Matthew, Mark, Luke and John written in those early years of Christianity.

Doesn't the same thing happen today? Some person makes the news. Her picture appears on television and the newspapers and magazines around the world. Everyone is talking about her. Larry King makes every effort to get an interview. People want to know what others think of the person, so that they can form an opinion for themselves.

In reading the New Testament, especially the four gospels and the Letters of Paul, I keep on hearing one question: "What do I think about Jesus?"

There are three kinds of Christians: those who are Christians in name only, who have "dropped out" of the Christian life by decision or indecision; those who follow Christ with a Low Christology; and those who follow him with a High Christology.

Obviously there are Buddhists and people of other non-Christian religions, or those with no religion at all, who are not going to follow Jesus in the way Christians are being called to follow Jesus.

What am I talking about? What's "Christology?"

"Logy" as in psychology, sociology, biology, anthropology, means "words" or "study" about some subject or topic. It's from the Greek word "logos" meaning "word."

Christology simply means words or *study* about Christ.

Describing someone as having a "Low Christology" is not a put-down.

A person with a *Low Christology* would be someone who sees Jesus as a great Wisdom Teacher—and/or as a loving, compassionate person—one of the best who ever lived—but not as someone to relate to as God.

H.G. Wells, views Jesus with a *Low Christology*. He sees him as having had the most influence on our world—especially in the Western world. His stress is Jesus, the great teacher, great Wisdom figure, person with great compassion, a revolutionary who changed people's fundamental attitudes.

Wells writes, "Of course the reader and I live in countries where to millions of persons, Jesus is more than a man. But the historian must disregard that fact. He must adhere to the evidence that would pass unchallenged if his book were to be read in every nation under the sun. Now, it is interesting and significant that a historian, without any theological bias whatever, should find that he cannot portray the progress of humanity honestly without giving a foremost place to a penniless teacher from Nazareth. The old Roman historians ignored Jesus entirely; he left no impress on the historical records of his time. Yet, more than 1900 years later, a historian like myself, who does not even call himself a Christian, finds the picture centering irresistibly around the life and character of this most significant man."

This is clearly *Low Christology*. Wells stresses Jesus' personal magnetism— so powerful that it induced people "who had seen him only once to leave their business and follow him." He points out that Jesus' teachings and his outlook challenge not only individuals, but also institutions to change their attitude and ways of dealing with people. Jesus stressed understanding, tolerance, good will, and the call for a universal brotherhood and sisterhood.

In 1925, an advertising man, Bruce Barton, came out with a life of Jesus that sold over a half-million copies, *"The Man Nobody Knows."* I've read it at least five times. He presents Jesus in a unique way, as unique as in the play *Godspell* or the musical *Jesus Christ Superstar* or the movie, *Jesus of Nazareth*.

Barton, one of the founders and later chairman of the board of the advertising firm of Batten, Barton, Durstine and Osborne, wrote a great advertisement for Jesus. It worked. He advertised Jesus well. He presents a *Low Christology*.

His hope was that people would *not* see Jesus as a weak and meek "Lamb of God", but rather as a powerful person who changed history. They would regard him as a model to imitate; a leader, a sociable person, aware of others, forgiving, teaching, reaching out, challenging, and compassionate.

A *Low Christology* presents Jesus with high marks in many areas, inspiring people to read his life and practice what he preached.

The Jewish writer, Sholem Asch wrote, "Jesus Christ is the outstanding personality of all time . . . No other teacher—Jewish, Christian, Buddhist, Mohammedan—is *still* a teacher whose teaching is such a guidepost for the world we live in. Other teachers may have something basic for an Oriental, an Arab, or an Occidental; but every act and word of Jesus has value for all of us. He became the Light of the World. Why shouldn't I, a Jew, be proud of that?"

Bruce Barton's book, *The Man Nobody Knows,* ends with Jesus dying on the cross.

High Christology begins with Jesus rising from the dead.

That requires a "leap of faith". It's says that Jesus is different from Gandhi and Bruce Barton and Paul and Aristotle.

To move from a *Low Christology* to a *High Christology* means making a move into the Divine.

If I move from a *Low Christology* to a *High Christology*, I'll see Jesus as God. I'll be saying, "Jesus is my Savior." I'll be proclaiming, "Jesus is Lord."

If I move from a *Low Christology* to a *High Christology*, I will be moving into a relationship with Jesus, prayer with him, spirituality, mysticism, commitment, communion.

Moving from a *Low Christology* to a *High Christology*, I will be seeing people in a different way, as the Body of Christ.

Now obviously there are degrees of how one sees and relates to Jesus. Moreover, people fluctuate. Relationships develop and relationships disintegrate. There are degrees in a *Low* and a *High* Christology. Theologians would be adding "er's" to Low and High, talking about "Lower" and "Higher" Christologies.

It's practical to present just two positions when it comes to Christology. Stark contrasts sometimes help. Jesus as teacher often did just that, talking about being either a sheep or a goat, a wise virgin or a foolish one, walking the narrow way or the broad way, being a dead tree or a live tree, being a wise servant or a lazy one.

Christians with a *High Christology* are happy when others see Jesus as a great teacher and wisdom figure, as well as a great human being.

If one wants to clearly grasp these distinctions, the book to read is *Mere Christianity* by C.S. Lewis.

I'm willing to bet that this book by C.S. Lewis will be around and used for the next five hundred years. H.G. Wells and Bruce Barton's words will disappear. Of course, I won't be around, so if I'm not worried about losing my bet. I would also vote for *Mere Christianity* to be labeled "The best Christian book of this century."

Mere Christianity appeared in 1943 and still sells copy after copy. If you haven't read it yet, look for this paperback in any book store. You might accuse me of having a hidden agenda—trying to win my bet by keeping sales running high.

It's catechism. Theology. Ethics. Creed. It's worth taking a chapter at a time and struggling with his description of what is basic to all Christians: *Mere Christianity*. It's clear and it's tough. It will get you thinking.

It's the result of Lewis' personal evolution from no faith to becoming a Christian. It's the result of his study and thinking and thrashing out Christian theology in order to give radio talks in the first half of the 1940's. *Mere Christianity* is a short book with quick meaty chapters.

Concerning Christology, Lewis writes, "For when you get down to it, is not the popular idea of Christianity simply this: that Jesus Christ was a great moral teacher and that if only we took his advice we might be able to establish a better social order and avoid another war? Now, mind you, that is quite true. But it tells you much less than the whole truth about Christianity and it has no practical importance at all."

Lewis then points out that if we followed Plato or Aristotle or Confucius, the world would also be a better place. But people don't do that. "Why are we more likely to follow Christ than any of the others? Because he is the best moral teacher? But that makes it even less likely that we shall follow him. If we cannot take the elementary lessons, is it likely we are going to take the most advanced ones. If Christianity only means one more bit of good advice, then Christianity is of no importance. There has been no lack of good advice for the past four thousand years. A bit more makes no difference."

Obviously, C.S. Lewis is saying that Christianity is about *High Christology*— which means that Jesus is the Son of God.

And he says more. He says "The Son of God became a man to enable men (and women) to become Sons (and Daughters) of God."

A man came to me one day and asked, "Why don't more priests use the word 'Jesus' when they talk about Jesus Christ?" This was a new question for me, so I asked what he meant. "Well," he said, "I listen to priests. Those who seem to have a personal relationship with Jesus call him 'Jesus.' Those who don't, seem to only call him 'Christ' when they preach—as in 'Christ said this' or 'Christ did that.'"

I said, "Oh." Then after what must have seemed like ages, I added, "I don't know." I don't know. It seemed "judgmental." I suppose the place to start is to know oneself better and if and what my relationship with Jesus is like.

I know that people like Nicodemus in the Gospel of John needed time to develop a relationship with Jesus.

I know that Jesus was a carpenter with words and he urges us to build the foundation of our life on his words and on him.

Saint Ignatius of Loyola, the founder of the Jesuits, was wounded in battle and asked for some romantic novels for reading during his recovery. Instead he was given *Lives of the Saints* and a *Life of Christ*. This reading about Jesus and the saints was a struggle, but afterwards he felt peace. Reading trash was a pleasure, but afterwards he felt sleazy. In this basic human experience he discovered the principle of discernment. In this basic human experience, he figured out that a relationship with Jesus was what his life was all about.

Saint Alphonsus Liguori wrote over a hundred books, but the three things he wrote that really touched the common folk were: *The Practice of The Love of Jesus Christ, The Stations of the Cross,* and his *Visits to Jesus in the Blessed Sacrament.* All three urge a deep relationship with Jesus. For the past two and a half centuries, Catholics have sat in churches before a tabernacle where they believe Jesus Christ is present, and there they have prayed to him. They have walked around inside church buildings using Saint Alphonsus' short *"Stations of the Cross"* to help them in praying to Jesus as they meditate on Jesus' journey to Calvary. They have read the book, *The Practice of the Love of Jesus Christ,* in which Alphonsus states right from the beginning: "The whole sanctity and perfection of a person consists in loving Jesus Christ."

I'm not the type to push in your face books or pieces of cardboard with Bible texts, telling you what you have to do to be saved, that you have to proclaim Jesus as your Lord and Savior. I hope everyone has a personal experience with Jesus as I have had in my life, and even deeper. It's been my experience that people will discover Jesus when they discover Jesus.

Some will meet Jesus at work, like Matthew. Some will meet him at night like Nicodemus. Some will meet him at the well, like the Samaritan woman. Some will meet him when they are being attacked by others, like the woman caught in adultery. Some will meet him when filled with self-righteousness and then hit bottom, like Paul.

Some will meet him quietly in prayer, as I first did. As a result of that experience, I love Jesus. As a result of that experience, I keep meeting him in the poor and the rich, the sick and the healthy, the young and the old, and so many in between. I have sat with him in prayer these past thirty-eight years, and have tried to live with him and with his principles in my life.

That's my Christology, my words, thoughts and feelings about Jesus Christ.

Aristotle:
For Dummies

*B*esides Jesus and Buddha, H.G. Wells also mentions Aristotle (384-322 B.C) —and in that order—as one of the three most influential persons in history.

Aristotle?

What about Plato, Albert Einstein, or Roger Bacon? What about great thinkers, philosophers and inventors from the Orient, Australia, Russia or other places in the world that have had pivotal influences on all of us? Was H.G. Wells being myopic?

Aristotle?

I can see why Jesus and Buddha made his list, but I wondered how Aristotle has influenced our world and my life.

An answer: he stressed the need for system, method, scientific research, questions, focus, clarity, logic, definition, and making distinctions. He stressed the need for clear thinking.

Clarity, system, method, organization, thoroughness . . .

Isn't that what we hope for from those who produce hamburgers? Or from medical labs dealing with our body and our blood? Isn't that what we want from those who give us news or make legislative decisions? Isn't that what we want from the pulpit and the podium, from our preachers and our teachers, from those flying the plane we're in, from the person servicing our car and city, protecting us from breakdowns and break-ins?

We want system, logic, clarity, definition and distinctions.

We want to know causes, so that we can understand effects.

We demand it of others. Do we demand it of ourselves?

At Alcoholics Anonymous they say: "Beware of stinking thinking."

Remember IBM's motto, "Think."

Aristotle would stress the gathering of information and the studying of that information. "Facts! Give me the facts." One can study, think and reason with *facts*. Before you make a statement, check everything out. Do your homework. Do it neatly. Line up everything that pertains to the case. Observe appearances and then get beneath and beyond appearances.

I did my homework. I went to libraries and read all I could read by and about Aristotle. I typed in the word, "Aristotle" on the search slot on the Internet. Surprise! There were over 18,000 references to Aristotle. I checked many of them, taking notes and thinking about what I read. It brought me back to the courses I had in college philosophy and the history of philosophy.

Research demands the hard work of gathering data. Watching a trial shows us how important detailed detective work can be. When testifying and trying to give exact times, dates, places, and other details, there are two kinds of witnesses: those who try to be scrupulously honest in giving details and those who are not.

There are two kinds of people in general: the poetic and the analytical. One sees that "The fog comes / on little cat feet. / It sits looking / over the harbor and city / on silent haunches / and then moves on." (Carl Sandburg) Another turns on the Weather Channel to see where this messy weather is coming from.

I would guess that Carl Jung's most popular book is *Psychological Types*. I've looked up things in it over and over again. Often, when I pick it up, I notice a long quotation he cites, just before his Introduction. It's a statement on Plato and Aristotle from the German poet and critic, Heinrich Heine (1797-1856):

> *"Plato and Aristotle! These are not merely two systems, they are types of two distinct human natures, which from time immemorial, under every sort of disguise, stand more or less inimically opposed. The whole medieval world in particular was riven by this conflict, which persists down to the present day, and which forms the most essential content of the history of the Christian Church. Although under other names, it is always of Plato and Aristotle that we speak. Visionary, mystical, Platonic natures disclose Christian ideas and the corresponding symbols from the fathomless depths of their souls. Practical, orderly, Aristotelian natures build out of these ideas and symbols a fixed system, a dogma, and a cult. Finally the Church embraces both natures, one of them entrenched in the clergy and the other in monasticism, but both keeping up a constant feud."* (Deutschland)

A building contractor once complained to me about an architect: "If he had to construct this building, he would never have put in all these twists and turns, curves and corners."

Many couples argue over the way they deal differently with their children. One is all heart; the other all mind. A father lays down a principle that seems cold and cruel to one of the kids, who then comes crying to Mother.

A principal of a school follows the principle: "No favorites. All are treated equally around here." In fact, that statement is on a poster on her office wall. She becomes upset when one of her teachers plays favorites, wants special privileges, or doesn't follow rules made at faculty meetings. The teacher responds by spreading statements like, "The principal is so cold. She doesn't have a heart."—Words that would hurt anyone who tries to work by principles.

Aristotle was lucky. When he came to Athens in his late teens, he had a teacher named Plato. It's fortunate when you have a great teacher who has gifts you don't have.

People often marry their opposites.

Kids need parents who are different from each other.

Presidents, governors, mayors, bishops, managers, had better not be surrounded with "yes people" or "clones." They'd better have their opposites and plenty of opposition.

Plato had Socrates. But their differences were nothing compared to the differences between Plato and Aristotle.

Plato had experience. Aristotle was green. Plato, some forty years older, was in the Autumn of his life. Aristotle was in his Spring. Plato stressed stepping back and entering into contemplation. Aristotle preferred jumping in and then observing. As a result of the mix, Aristotle learned a bit about the mystical, not just the physical, the soul, not just the body, the beautiful, not just the factual.

In her book, *The Echo of Greece,* Edith Hamilton writes, "Through Plato, Aristotle came to believe in God, but Plato never attempted to prove His reality. Aristotle had to do so. Plato contemplated Him; Aristotle produced arguments to demonstrate Him. Plato never defined Him, but Aristotle thought God through logically and concluded with entire satisfaction to himself that He was the Unmoved Mover. Plato said, 'To find the Father and Creator of all is hard, and having found Him it is impossible to utter him.' Mystery Aristotle rejected."

Plato taught Aristotle that there is an "Unmoved Mover" beneath all that moves. Edith Hamilton puts it this way: Plato taught Aristotle to speak "of the voice of the God within us."

I remember hearing an interesting anecdote about an orange. A teacher gave an assignment to her Science Class to come to class the next day prepared to *describe an orange*. One student stood up and told about where oranges grow, and what kind of climate they need. Another told about the orange's chemistry. Another told the reason for its color. Then one student went to the front of the room, took an orange in her hands, bit into it and said, "Ummm"!

If the teacher was grading her students, how would they be marked? I think it would depend on whether the teacher was a disciple of Plato or Aristotle.

Aristotle would want to know everything physical about the orange: its variations, type, etc., as well as its contents. Plato would be fascinated by the delicious flavor, the roundness, and the beautiful color of this orange— and all oranges.

There are facts and there are mysteries, those who are practical and those who are mystical.

In history and in fashion, opposites sometimes beget opposites. A period of romanticism is often followed by a period of rationalism which is followed by a period of romanticism.

Obviously we need both. Obviously, Aristotle had a profound influence on our world with his stress on the need to be rational, to study the way animals, vegetables and things of this earth are.

Present or Absent?

One of the qualities that Jesus, the Buddha, and Aristotle had was presence. They were present to the world and the people that surrounded them.

Some people say "present" when they are really absent.

Some musicians play a piece of music as if it was for the first time; others are playing somewhere else.

Some actors in a Broadway production play their 423rd performance with the same freshness as opening night.

Some people actually see a banana cream pie. Then they taste its sweetness and savor its "ummm." Some people don't see the banana cream pie. All they see is calories. All they taste is guilt. They wonder and worry about what people around them are thinking about them as they eat it.

Some people stay on their honeymoon for the rest of their lives. Their marriage keeps getting better and better. For others, the honeymoon ends about 116 weeks later—more or less.

Some people see only generalities, numbers, objects, shapes, categories, sexes. Other people see Patty and Molly and George and Pat and Mike and that the color of the walls in the living room of their cousin's house is a different shade of beige than the beige in the family room where there is an old Philco radio with one knob missing.

Some people hear dentist office music.

Some people can sense loneliness in another, almost as well as a person with arthritis can tell the weather is about to change.

Some people at a basketball game observe how various basketball players shoot their foul shots differently. They notice how two players guard the same player differently. They watch how the way the assistant coach on one team is always looking and checking the head coach, while the assistant coach on the other bench is jotting something down on paper after each play. Other people just sit there enjoying everyone and everything that surrounds them: the hot dogs, fans doing the wave, clapping, booing, laughing, getting up and down to let people go by them who have to go to the rest room or get more food or use the telephone.

Some people at a baseball game watch the game on the field and some watch the people in the stands. Some people watch their watches, yawn, and are thinking about a meeting they have to attend the next morning. Do season ticket holders watch a game differently from people who are seeing their very first major league baseball game?

Some people at meetings don't hear anything anyone is saying because they're spending the whole time planning and rehearsing what they are going to say when they raise their hand to make a comment about what someone said thirty-five minutes earlier.

Some parents actually experience the birth of their third child with a deeper wonder than the birth of their firstborn. Others say that there is nothing like the birth of their first child.

Some people attend church services worrying about whether there is going to be any rye bread left at the bakery when they stop in there on the way home from church.

Some people stand in front of us and talk at us, while their eyes are watching someone on the other side of the room or they're talking to themselves about something that person did to them last week.

Some joggers, in spite of rumors to the contrary, smile while they jog. They're having the time of their life.

Some people enjoy every plane ride with the same excitement as their first.

Some people actually listen to what we're saying. In fact, they ask questions about something we've said, to make sure they understand what we mean.

Some people taste the second piece of pizza.

Some people pray, without words, without an agenda, sitting there in silence, in love, in the presence of a loving God.

Some people enjoy driving within the speed limit—without having to pass people, without having to high-beam people who don't turn down their bright lights as they come toward them in the night, who don't have to honk or curse or make gestures.

Some people talk to waiters or waitresses and begin by asking their name.

Some people can applaud spontaneously even if they are the only one to clap and nobody else joins in.

Some people cry during the evening news, every time they see the homeless and the starving babies. They never seem to become insensitive to the poor and forgotten.

Some people, as Jesus tells us, take time to watch the birds of the sky. They bird-watch. They love to see formations of birds flying north and south in Spring and in Autumn. They know all the birds by name that stay in their neighborhood. They love to see birds fly and dive. They notice birds building nests and planning for their new arrivals. They stop to watch a blackbird who has stopped to watch them from a high branch.

Some people, who never see birds, love to go to air shows. They love to watch all kinds of planes being rolled out and taking off and flying. They enjoy seeing planes flying in precise formation across the sky.

Some pro-life people are truly pro-life. They see the sacredness of *all* life. They visit nursing homes. They volunteer in soup kitchens. They worry about a thirteen-year-old girl who uses sex for self-esteem with an eighteen-year-old boy who uses her for sex. They pray and meditate about their own life.

Some people live life to the full; some don't.

Blurts

Do you blurt?

I do.

I suspect everybody does.

Blurts are those short, sudden, sort of semi-loud exclamations we make to ourselves when we finally figure something out.

We let out a blurt when we gain an insight into something good or something bad. Sometimes blurts are complaints or gripes or curses or questions. They are the "finale" to something we were talking to ourselves about that we might not have known we were thinking about.

"What?"

That could be a blurt—that is, if you were trying to figure out what I was saying as you were reading.

In fact, I'd be glad if you said "What?" If you didn't, maybe you'd be like me at times. With book in hand, I read along, but my mind is elsewhere, because the writer hasn't grabbed me.

It's not a new word. Webster says the English word "blurt" dates back to 1573, then gives a definition of the word.

Blurts are abrupt utterances.

Sometimes they are impulsive, inadvertent or ill-advised.

Blurts may signify low-grade insights or steps toward an important discovery.

High-grade insights we announce to those around us.

Low-grade blurts we keep to ourselves.

"What was that you just muttered, Honey?"

"Oh nothing. I was just talking to myself."

Here are some of my recent blurts. If you resonate with any of these, you might let out a blurt of your own such as, "Oh *that's* what he's talking about."

- "Okay."
- "Oh yeah!"
- "So that's the way it works!"
- "I should have known."
- "That's life!"
- "Aaaah! How could I be so stupid?"
- "I'm out of here."
- "Never again."
- "I blew that one."
- "How dumb can I be?"
- "I guess my expectations weren't their expectations."
- "Uhhhhhhhhhhhhhhhhhhhhhhhhhhhhh!"
- "This happens every time."
- "When am I ever going to learn?"
- "#*&8!!!#/*!"

- "Same to you, Buddy!"
- "Ugh! I'm my own worst enemy."
- "That's what it's all about."
- "The clock is ticking."
- "Oh no!"
- "Help!"
- "Thank You, God."

Do you blurt?

I do.

Truck Driver: Right?

I drive a truck.

People think I'm dumb—not stupid—but dumb. There is a difference between being dumb and being stupid.

Right?

Dumb is being foolish, silly, dizzy or inane. Naive.

Stupid? Well, to earn that description, you have to be thick-headed, unteachable, dull or dense.

So, why do people think I'm dumb?

I'm a truck driver. That's all. That's it.

People think truck drivers are dumb.

Well, not everyone. Some of those who don't think truck drivers are dumb, may not think about truck drivers at all. They just don't notice them.

Other people who don't think truck drivers are dumb are their families— and other truck drivers.

Sometimes this bothers me. Most of the time it doesn't. I just keep driving along doing my own job.

It all started when I went for my first interview after college. I had a degree. I had the smarts. I got the job. Then they told me that I'd have to wear a suit—preferably, a dark blue suit—with a white or light blue shirt—dark tie—it could have stripes.

I could wear a short-sleeved shirt in summer, but I had to wear that tie around my neck and had to have a jacket nearby, just in case.

Well, I didn't take that job, or the next one, or the one after that.

Now my parents and my brother still think I'm "dumb" for refusing all these "good jobs" because I didn't want to wear a suit. They say I should have thought about this before going to college. But my mother and father pushed me to go.

I don't regret having gone to college. I had a good time and a few good courses. I learned a lot. But stuck for money, stuck for a tieless job, it was time to try trucking.

I discovered that I liked it. Better: I loved it.

So that's what I've been doing for the past twenty years.

It's been quite a trip. It's been a real education. I've been able to see the great big USA: Route 80 coast to coast. Route 85, 81; 75, 65, north to south. Routes 90, 70, 40, 10, 46, 66, 76. You name it. I've traveled it.

After I married, when I had seniority, I was able to stay closer to home. Family is more important than freedom.

My wife and kids have someone who is happy and who is there, never too far away. And I know the best spots for vacations.

Medical benefits: good. And good money if you want to put in the hours. But life is more than money.

Payoffs and perks? You can't think of work only in bottom-line terms: "What do you make?" Obviously, the best things in life are priceless. The country western songs and the Jesus songs that I hear on the radio keep saying that.

Driving across the country, coming out of the night, driving around a bend, seeing the sun rise in the east, and photographing it with my eyes, all priceless.

Going through rain, passing lakes, rivers, even the ocean in some spots. I love to see water. And later the rushing wash of hot water on my back when taking a refreshing shower after a long roll down many roads. Now that's living.

Honking my horn for a van with kids and picturing one of them elbowing a brother and a sister and saying to their parents, "Dad! Mom! That's five truck drivers in a row that honked their horns for me. I've got the secret!" They don't. I have kids. But they don't know that I check all around me first to make sure that I'm not going to cause an accident. Sometimes I don't honk. Traffic's too tight. Yet, I'm still a kid. I love to honk for a kid, especially when it looks like it's the younger brother who is doing the signaling. I was the younger brother.

Utah? Have you ever seen Utah? Don't miss it. Idaho too, and West Virginia, and Western North Carolina. Have you ever seen Western North Carolina? The coast is great, but too much traffic.

Now, of course, you can see all this from the sky by airplane, but have you ever crossed them driving coast to coast? What I'm getting at is the thrill of driving along and seeing great spots for the first time: Chicago, San Francisco, British Columbia, the Rockies, the Great Lakes, the Smokies, certain hills in Pennsylvania along Route 80, the Delaware Gap, the deserts of New Mexico, Arizona and California . . .

Dumb? I don't think so.

Stupid? Certainly not.

There's so much to see: I'll keep on trucking.

Life's Bottom Lines

Benjamin Disraeli: "The two greatest stimulants in the world are love and debt."

Margaret Mitchell: "Death and taxes and childbirth! There's never any convenient time for any of them."

Bill Cosby: "I don't know the key to success, but the key to failure is trying to please everybody."

Ann Morrow Lindbergh: "One cannot collect all the beautiful shells on the beach."

O. Henry: "Life is made up of sobs, sniffles, and smiles, with sniffles predominating."

Naomi Judd: "Slow down, simplify and be kind."

Franz Kafka: "The meaning of life is that it stops."

Albert Einstein: "Only a life lived for others is the life worth while."

Jesus Christ: "Greater love than this no one has, that they lay down their life for their friends."

Elmer Davis: "The first and great commandment is, Don't let them scare you."

Logan Pearsall Smith: "There are two important things to aim at in life: first to get what you want; and after that, to enjoy it. Only the wisest of mankind achieve the second."

Lao Tzu: "The world is ruled by letting things take their course."

T.S. Eliot: "Birth, and copulation, and death / That's all the facts when you / come down to brass tacks."

Tennessee Williams: "Most peoples lives—what are they but trails of debris, each day more debris, more debris, long, long trails of debris with nothing to clean it all up but, finally death?"

Harry S. Truman: "Three things ruin a man. Power, money, and women. I never wanted power. I never had any money, and the only woman in my life is up at the house right now."

Willa Cather wrote, "There are only two or three human stories, and they go on repeating themselves as fiercely as if they had never happened before."

Basho, the Japanese poet: "It is evening, autumn; / I think only / Of my parents."

Henry David Thoreau: "You must get your living by loving."

Anna Quindlen: "The life you have led doesn't need to be the only life you have."

Mary Roberts Rinehart: "A little work, a little sleep, a little love and it's all over."

John, Viscount Morley of Blackburn: "The great business of life is to be, to do, to do without, and to depart."

Thornton Wilder wrote, "My advice to you is not to inquire why or whither, but just enjoy your ice cream while it's on your plate—that's my philosophy."

Gilda Radner: "I wanted a perfect ending . . . Now I've learned, the hard way, that some poems don't rhyme, and some stories don't have a clear beginning, middle and end. Life is about not knowing, having to change, taking the moment and making the best of it, without knowing what's going to happen next. Delicious ambiguity."

Space

*S*omeone said, "Whenever you see a Chinese painting, look at the empty spaces. You'll see a lot more."

Is that true?

I don't know.

I haven't really looked at too many Chinese paintings.

But I have stood on docks and the decks of boats and looked into dark waters. And there have been times at night when I have stood my ground and gazed into space—into the high night sky—and closed my eyes and wandered into the depths of my own being, into my emptiness. And sometimes, only sometimes, I've met God waiting for me there, in my emptiness.

I love airports. They're a great place for watching—watching people watching each other, watching people waiting. Watching people hugging one another because they are leaving for a while and watching people hugging each other because they've come home for a while.

Arrivals and departures.

I love airplanes—always asking for the window seat—watching clouds, watching the down below—also wondering about all the people around me—especially the person next to me—here in this space that surrounds us.

But more than planes, I love buses and trains—window seat again if possible—quietly sitting there—not having the stress and the cramp of driving in traffic—noticing people walking, talking, on the street, wondering about the people in the brown and tan house there, observing a guy leaning into a car talking to a girl who is on a cellular phone, watching a teenage boy on a skate board, seeing a kid by herself in a green-grass-yard practicing with a hula hoop—people twisting and turning and spinning along within the space of their lives.

Space—the emptiness, the fullness, the in-between of persons, places, things, homes, highways, mall parking lots . . .

Space—filled with so many scenes and so many people and so many things.

Space: filled with music and talk shows and sports and news. All we have to do is turn on the radio—AM, FM.

Space: where we can also shut off the sounds and be ever so silent.

Empty spaces can make a lot of noise.

Loneliness can be very loud.

Relationships can be very silent.

People are always moving closer or away from each other—sometimes quite dramatically, sometimes ever so slightly.

Giving each other space . . .

What isn't said, sometimes says so much more.

When it comes to space, there are three kinds of people:

1) The person who walks into a room and the room suddenly feels so empty;

2) The person who walks into a room and the room seems so filled with them. They take in all the air, causing suffo-cation, lumps in the throat, and some nervous twitching. We look at our watches. We want to run, to escape, to be out of there—anywhere—but there in their presence—in their space.

3) The person who gives *us* space, plenty of space, freedom. When they walk into our space, we relax. They listen. We listen. We experience communion. Smiles beget smiles. Time is forgotten. They breathe peace. Joy abounds. Joy surrounds us. They bring so much laughter and life and joy into our space.

Space.

How much space do I need?

Who has space for me in their space? Who wants me in? Who wants me out?

What happens when I walk into a room? What happens when I leave?

Where and how do I find space?

What are my escapes?

Escapes—my space walks—my ways of finding space—tricks of the trade: grabbing a book; picking up a newspaper; turning on the television; looking at my watch; "Up the down staircase;" "I have a meeting;" the bathroom; the back door; picking up dishes; turning out lights; turning my back on another.

What do I see when I look into space?

The eyes have it. Looks can kill. Looks can comfort. Looks can heal.

What shall I say?

Words: words spoken, words not spoken. Recognition? Rejection?

What are my signals?

Gestures: hands held in pockets; hands reaching out; kids hugged; kids not hugged; stepping back and holding the door for another.

My days . . .

How and with what do I fill these empty boxes called "my days"—those spaces on my kitchen calendar and in my appointment book?

I look back at the moments that make my day, that fill my calendar, that take time: the "Good morning!" kiss; the taste of orange juice on my tongue; pouring the cereal; handing someone a cup a coffee; "sugar?"; letting someone get ahead of me in traffic; getting into my work first thing in the morning; listening to someone at a coffee break—being quiet during their pauses; remembering to make an important phone call; a smile; making supper; driving a kid to basketball practice; bringing out the garbage; stopping to chat with a neighbor walking his dog; volunteering to help someone learn to read; handing another the TV clicker; lowering the volume so someone can sleep; the embrace. A full day.

Other days seem slow: "I feel like I'm stuck in space. Dead before I'm dead." It happens. People get stuck—stuck in a relationship that isn't moving. Something has died. Someone has died. It's frozen love. We're like barges locked in ice for the winter, the long winter of cold silence. Stuck in frozen, non-moving space. Painful . . .

Stop the world, I want to get off.

Stop the music.

Stop the merry-go-round.

And then the baby cries. She wants food. She wants to see someone, to be held, to feel skin, to see a face. She wants someone in her space.

Or I see the phone. I wonder if someone will call.

Or I see the door. I wonder when another will arrive.

If someone comes, I'll no longer be alone. Another will be in my empty space with me.

Or I go to the store and buy the latest "toy" to fill my empty space or I eat and drink too much. Maybe this will fill my empty space.

Space.

"When you see a Chinese painting, look at the empty spaces. You'll see a lot more"?

I don't know.

I'll have to find some space and look into it.

The Wind

Sitting on a rock, on top of a hill, alone, leaning against a tree, looking into the early Autumn air . . .

The wind blows where it wills: along the fields, into a grove of trees, shaking the leaves, millions of orange, red, yellow, tan, and some still green leaves, twisting, shaking, looking like a park full of kids on rides, flying, spinning through the air, round and round, shrieking with laughter. And I sit here worrying about tomorrow.

The wind blows where it wills: across my face, cooling my being, lowering the Indian Summer temperature. And I sit here going over what happened last week, last year, twenty, thirty, forty years ago.

The wind blows: soft and cool in the springtime of life, hot, sticky, sometimes still, sometimes stormy, our youth, picking up speed in the Autumn of life and then the wild, raging, but sometimes stopped, dead wind in the Winter of life.

The wind blows where it wills . . .

Come Spirit of God. Breathe new life into me. Make me see that this moment on this hill, is where you want to form me anew. Each now, whether in the morning, noon, or evening of my life, can be my moment of new birth.

You want me. You created me. You invite me to wake with you in the morning, work with you in the day, and walk with you in the cool of the evening.

But like Adam and Eve, I too often notice myself hiding.

Like Ezekiel's vision of the dry bones, I also see that parts of me are scattered all over the place.

Lord, God, walk this earth again. Call me once again, "Where are you?"

Reach down, reform this earth, this clay body of mine, and breathe new life into me.

Send prophets to wail over my dry bones that I may rise.

Send your son to shout at the rock that locks me in, "Lazarus come forth."

Jesus, walk across the waters of my life, through the storm, and challenge me to walk across the waters toward you. Let me hear your words, "Peace, be still."

Father, Son, send your Holy Spirit into my Upper Room. Shake my house down to its foundations.

Rebuild me on your rock!

Jesus, Carpenter, worker with wood and word, high on a hill, hanging forever above the world on the Wood of the cross, call me to Calvary, to sit beneath your cross, to ponder these great truths—to feel the Wind, the breath of your Spirit.

Sitting on a rock, on top of a hill, alone, leaning against a tree, looking into the early autumn air . . .

Two Women

We all meet lots of people along the way. Why do some stand out and some end hidden in the basement of our memory?

There was a nursing home I often visited a long time ago. I've forgotten everyone in that place but Delores and Annie—two women—both in their 80's and both widows.

Except for that, they were quite different.

Annie in the A Wing was a nervous wreck. Every time I visited her, she would ask, "Am I going to hell?" I failed in every attempt to assure her that she was not.

I lost every time. And I don't like to lose in anything, especially in the issue of hope. I've heard too many stories from people about something they were taught in their childhood that ruined their whole lives.

Where do you turn when there's no place to turn?

"Am I going to hell?"

Driving home, the echo of her fear, would always set me wondering, "What put into her mind that she was going to hell? Was it a sermon? Was it something she did—a sin, a disaster? Was it one thing? Was it many things? Was it anything?"

I never got the answer to any of those questions.

Delores in the D Wing was just the opposite. She had two months to live. That's what she told me her "cancer doctor" told her.

She told me that just after I visited Annie. I must have been brooding over her haunting question, "Am I going to hell?" So I asked Delores if she was scared.

"Scared?" She looked at me as if I had asked her if she was pregnant at eighty four. Then she smiled, seeing that my face was a bit red with embarrassment. "No, I'm not scared. I'm elated. Just think: in less than a two months I'll be looking into the smiling, radiant face of God."

Whoa! Silence.

Driving home I'd found myself saying, "What put into her mind that she was going to see the radiant face of God after she died? Where did she get such faith? Was it a sermon? Was it an experience? Was it her upbringing at home. What was it?"

Delores died.

Annie died.

I thought to myself, "What would it be like to have had both these women in the same room?"

Through the years they and their words echo in my memory.

I sometimes wonder, "In my old age, which of the two will I be?"

The Red Wagon

*I*t was one of those stories you never forget. It was a Christmas story.

I heard the story during an afternoon of prayer and reflection for a Holy Name Society group. Most were sixty and older. We were in a downstairs hall under a church in a small town in northeastern Pennsylvania, just north of Scranton.

The afternoon schedule included two talks. However, I saw it mainly as an opportunity for a group of people to share their faith and tell how that faith shaped their life. Being in an atmosphere where people can really talk is something I love to hope happen.

Now, of course, I have often heard jokes and criticism from people who dislike being asked to share in small groups. Fortunately, this group was willing to do whatever I asked. So I suggested small group sharing.

I hear some remarkable stories when people share their faith.

We arranged our fourteen chairs in a circle where we could all see and hear each other well.

I told the men, "I always learn a lot from listening to people's life experiences. Feel free to answer or just listen. First question: 'Can you recall a moment in your life when you knew that God was definitely with you?' Look back into your life and pick out a moment when you knew God was there, that God loved you, that God helped you, that God did something for you."

I then asked everyone to take a few minutes of silence to pray, to reflect, to remember such moments.

Silence. Profound silence.

Then we went around the circle, men telling stories from their lives. It was calm and very serious. Everyone listened.

Some told about moments in the Second World War. Others told about dangerous times in the nearby coal mines. Then came the story of The Red Wagon from about the sixth man in the circle to speak.

The story-teller was in his eighties, a giant of a man. He wore a plaid shirt, red suspenders, and a very happy face. He began, "To me the moment God was with us is obvious. It happened many years ago when our only child, Johnny, was five years of age."

That's how the man in the plaid shirt began his story, the story of his only child, Johnny, and the red wagon. Almost immediately tears came to his eyes.

"It was during the Depression. Just before Christmas. We were poor, very poor. My wife and I were planning to go into town a week before Christmas to take Johnny with us to the different stores. Our hope was that he would see a toy he'd like, but one that we could afford.

"Well, we went into the first store, and there it was: the red wagon. Well, that was the only toy he saw that day. He had to have it. He wanted that red wagon for Christmas, and nothing else would do.

"We said to him, my wife and I, 'Johnny, we're sorry, but we just don't have the money to buy a toy like that. Getting a red wagon for Christmas, that's a rich kid's toy, and we're poor.'"

"Well, he didn't understand. He was only five years old. He kept saying, 'Why, why, why? Why can't I get a red wagon for Christmas?'"

"We said, 'Johnny, red wagons are very expensive. We just can't afford it.' And we kept on trying to get him to think about something else. No luck.

We took him to a second store. Still no luck. Then he said, 'Well, maybe Santa Claus can afford it.'

"We said, 'We don't think Santa Claus brings toys like that to poor people like us.'

"Then he said, 'We'll see.' He was such a smart kid.

"We went to other stores. No luck. All he could see was red: the red wagon for Christmas. The three of us finally went home feeling sad. All three of us wanted that red wagon.

"We had supper. Johnny finally went to bed after talking about the red wagon for a few more hours. Well, my wife and I sat there feeling horrible. Our plan had failed. Both of us felt bad, of course, but we both agreed we couldn't afford to buy him the red wagon. It was way beyond us.

"Suddenly, my wife snapped her fingers, stood up and went into the bedroom. A minute later she came out saying, 'We're getting him the red wagon.' I said, 'With what?' She said, 'With this' and handed me her $10 dollar gold piece.

"I said, 'Honey, we can't do this. Your grandfather gave you this when you were a little girl and you wanted to give it to Johnny's first child when Johnny grows up and gets married.'

"She answered, 'Look, it just sits there in my top drawer in a box. It's doing nothing. Nobody's using it. Johnny will get a lot more use out of a red wagon.'

"We got the red wagon. The next day I went into work and at lunch time I went to the bank and exchanged the $10 dollar gold coin. After work I bought the red wagon. I brought it home and hid it in the garage, covering it with a tarp. Johnny didn't see it.

"For the next few days he kept on nagging us about the red wagon and we kept on saying that we couldn't afford such an expensive toy.

"Well, on Christmas morning, you should have seen his face when he saw the red wagon. He lit up. He screamed. 'I told you Santa Claus could afford to bring me a red wagon.'

"It was the best Christmas we ever had."

"And he loved his red wagon. Every day for the next five months it was part of him."

"Then it happened. I was at work. My nephew came running into the shop yelling for me. I knew immediately that my son Johnny was dead. I just knew it."

"My nephew said, 'Johnny's hurt. They told me to rush down here to get you. You have to come home immediately. He was struck by lightning.' We rushed home, but I knew he was dead."

"I was right. He was dead. Our only child. It nearly killed us . . . "

Quiet.

Tears in the room.

"But what saved us was the red wagon. We kept it. It's still in our cellar at home. It became our symbol that God is with us."

More tears.

The man continued, "Isn't that what life is all about? Giving. Isn't that what marriage is all about? Giving. Isn't that what children are all about? Giving. To bring a child into the world, to see the joy in his face for those five months with his red wagon. It was all worth it. In time, we were able to heal a bit. In time we were able to thank God that we had the joy of Johnny for five and a half years and especially those last five months before he died."

More tears.

I heard that story a long time ago. Looking back now after many years, I don't remember much of what anyone else said that day, but I'm sure that everyone in that circle had been brought together in communion and faith by the story of "The Red Wagon."

I Don't Know

Once I was giving some talks at a religion workshop in Washington D.C. It was for Directors of Religious Education—from around the country.

I worked hard preparing material for the group.

At the first coffee break, a woman came up to me and said, "Do you know what you are doing?" She caught me. I answered an obvious, but rather hesitant, "Ye-esss!?" But there was half a question mark in my answer.

I really didn't know what I was doing. I didn't even know, that I didn't know, what I was doing. "Father, forgive me for I don't know what I am doing."

Now, of course, I thought I knew what I was doing. I had prepared, hadn't I? But looking back now, I really didn't know what I was doing. Looking back, I wish I had said, "No. Of course, I don't know what I'm doing." And maybe if I was flippant, I would add, "Who does?"

Now I'm older. Now I could say: "Who of us really knows what we're doing?"

Oops, I'd better add that I hope pilots and mechanics and brain surgeons know exactly what they are doing!

Yet I'll bet that sometimes they too say to themselves in the middle of everything, "I wonder what I'm doing here." And at other times, "It's been a long and winding road to where I am and how I got here. A road with many twists and turns—a road I didn't know I was on till I arrived."

When people marry and later divorce or when people switch jobs, don't they say, "Wow, when I made that decision, I must have been living in the land of make-believe, in the land of denial and delusion."?

Maureen McCann, an excellent speaker, often says, "Everything has three stages: illusion, disillusionment, decision."

People get married, take a job, or buy a house, assuming the other person, the job or the house to be what it isn't. Surprise. The honeymoon ends. The person at the next desk has big problems. The basement of the house leaks.

The Talmud says, "Teach thy tongue to say, 'I do not know.'" I've said that to myself a thousand times. I've taught my tongue to say it, even though I didn't realize it.

Somewhere else I read, "Don't write in your diary about what happened today. You won't know what happened till next week." And I add, "or perhaps next year."

I've heard thousands of sermons and speeches. I've been to all kinds of workshops. Sometimes weeks, months, or years later, I realize that something someone said in all that babble really hit home.

I suppose one trick would be to pause on a regular basis and write down in a diary or notebook the sayings and one-liners that have become quite significant to us.

Another trick would be to look back on our life and list key moments that we didn't know were key learning moments when we were going through them.

And I suppose, if we could, it would be a good move to thank those who've said significant things to us.

I don't know who that woman was who asked me the question, "Do you know what you are doing?" But if by chance you're reading this, "Thank you."

Hidden Treasure

Once upon a time a man had two sons. He loved the one and never really noticed the other.

Now, he could never admit that this was how he felt, but the servants noticed, and both brothers knew down deep that this was the case.

Fathers have favorites. It happens in almost every family.

The son he loved, his first-born, he favored all his life. He gave him the best of everything—coats of many colors, pearls of great price. He served him the best wine first.

The younger boy, timid, thin, and born with a deformed hand, was given nothing. He always sat alone in the back seat of the car, wore hand-me-down clothes, and growing up never even got a sip of his father's wine. He felt like he was his father's great disappointment.

Well, when the father died suddenly, it was no shock when the will was read. The older son got the family farm—rich soil—wheat fields that always produced thirty, sixty and hundredfold, wheat fields that were all wheat, no weeds, wheat fields that would fill the family barns to over-flowing and even more. In fact, this son found a set of plans that his father had drawn up for newer barns.

The younger son was mentioned in the will. He was given some desert land to the west of what was now the older brother's farm.

Fortunes change and stories change.

Some twenty years later, the younger son was the richest man in the country. He discovered a treasure in his empty fields: oil. There were millions and millions of barrels under his desert land.

There came a famine in that land. The rain seemed to stop and the wheat didn't bloom. The desert crawled closer and closer to the older brother's farm. Nothing grew on the land. And the older brother found himself starving. He longed to eat what his pigs used to eat.

Now, the younger brother, filled with compassion for his brother and his family invited him into partnership with him. He accepted. The older brother who had been dead began to come back to life.

At first he wouldn't come into the younger brother's house. He wasn't used to music and dancing. So the younger brother came out and embraced him and then brought him into his house. Slowly the brothers learned to know and love one another as they never had before.

Fortunes change and stories change.

Catch of the Day

I happened to meet her while drinking coffee before the beginning of a "Morning on Prayer" in the local parish hall. She had a nice smile, made quick funny comments, and seemed like a very interesting woman.

Her name was Maggie. It was printed boldly in blue marker on a white name tag. I'd guess she was somewhere between sixty and seventy.

The group that morning consisted of about thirty women and ten men. (Is that because men die earlier? Or is it because women are more interested in prayer? I don't know.) I had seen the notice in the diocesan paper, so I thought I'd attend to see what people were thinking and saying about prayer and I knew I could use a boost to my own prayer life.

Back to Maggie.

I asked her where she came from. She was originally from Michigan, but moved to this parish, where she was married forty years earlier. Then she asked me where I was from. However, I didn't get a chance to answer, because just then, the lady at the microphone started speaking, "May I have your attention please?"

Many kept talking—hearing and not hearing—enjoying the moment to chat, connect and confirm.

"May I have your attention please?"

She waited until everyone was silent. Then, as we stood there with our Styrofoam cups of coffee, she continued, "You'll notice on your name tags, there is a number. That's your table number; so now could you please go to your tables? Thanks."

There were lots of mumbled groans. Most people don't like being separated from friends. I guess a day like this was a day for connecting with each other, more than connecting with God. Or maybe this is the way many people connect with God. I don't know.

Finally, we were seated. I could still hear some grumblings about the seating arrangement. I could also read some slightly angry faces saying, "This better be good."

A nice surprise: Maggie was one of the four other persons at my table! We were three women and two men.

The woman in charge, the one woman at the podium, began, "Welcome to a 'Morning on Prayer' sponsored by the Spirituality Committee of Holy Spirit Parish. Our speaker this morning is Sister Teresa Grothaus." After indicating who and where Sister Teresa was, the woman looked at her script and continued, "Sister Teresa 'retired' ten years ago after 32 years in the classroom. She is now going to various parish groups speaking about prayer." She then looked up from her script and said, "We heard about Sister Teresa from the people at Holy Rosary Parish. They told us she was excellent! So I now give you Sister Teresa Grothaus."

Sister Teresa went to the mike and began by saying, "Thank you. Thank you for inviting me." She continued, "I'd like to begin with a prayer."

We all lowered our heads, which is the usual response whenever anyone says that. Sister Teresa had her head bowed too. I was observing all this. After about a minute of silence, she prayed, "Lord, teach us to see how we pray and how others pray. And Lord, teach us how you prayed." She then led us in the "Lord's Prayer."

Sister Teresa then spoke on prayer, with many examples, and gave us what was to be a marvelous morning. She was obviously a woman who prayed, and someone who wanted to help others pray.

What impressed me was her emphasis on the old principle, "Pray as you can; don't pray as you can't."

Looking back now from the distance of a few years, I realize that what really helped me most was something Maggie said. After a coffee break that nobody wanted to end, Sister Teresa announced from the microphone, "Your attention please . . . Your attention please . . . I'd like you to chat with the people at your table for the next half hour. I'd like to give everyone a chance to tell each other how you yourself already pray."

I suppose, from having done this many times, as well as from looking at some of the faces, she added, "Relax. You don't have to speak, if you don't want to. Just listen. However, it's been my experience that when the subject is prayer, everyone talks. People discover that everyone prays. People learn that we all pray in different ways. When we hear how others pray we become willing to talk about how we pray. And when we look at the way we pray, we pray even better—as well as beginning to try ways that we learn from others."

I don't know what the other three people at our table said that day, but I do remember what Maggie said. She taught me how to pray in a new way.

She said: "Every night before I go to bed, I just sit there in my favorite chair and think about the specifics of the day."

She leaned on that word "specifics."

"I sort of go fishing. I look for the 'catch of the day'—my favorite moment of the day."

Maggie's eyes were closed and her face was glowing as she gave some examples of what she meant.

"It might have been a call from someone trying to sell me something over the phone. I never buy anything that way, but I might ask the lady where she was calling from and we end up having a good conversation about the weather in Arizona. It might have been a chance meeting at the super-market where a neighbor showed me a photograph of her new granddaughter a thousand miles away. It might have been looking out the window and watching Billy, the kid across the street helping his baby sister

Kathy ride his bike. Or it might have been visiting my friend Sally, who is home-bound in a wheelchair, and having a nice cup of tea together with a piece of her wonderful peanut butter pie."

She became quiet and then added, "Then I thank God for my 'catch of the day.'"

That day she caught me. I've been doing the same thing ever since. It's a good night prayer. I find myself thanking God for specific people and moments in my day that tend to get lost in the rush and shuffle of life. And I've also noticed it's making me more aware of the specific people and moments of the next day.

And I've wondered from time to time, "On the night of our Prayer Day, when Maggie looked back over her day, was the time at our table, her best moment. Were we, who shared that special time with her, the 'catch of the day'?"

Snapshots:
On Being There

Not long ago my sister, Mary, was telling me about a September trip she and her husband, Gerry, took to Alaska. A couple of days later, I found myself still thinking about a comment she had made: "I think it's crazy for people to travel all the way to Alaska only to see the place through the lens of a camera. The first time they'll see it is when they get home and look at their pictures."

I found myself nodding "yes" and "no" to that observation, that judgment.

I also sensed she might be talking about me without knowing it.

Yes, it's probably true for some people. Their main goal is to see Alaska *for someone else.* "My friend couldn't make the trip, so I'll take Alaska back to her in pictures." Sort of like the same reason people buy T-shirts and souvenirs of a place or send post cards saying, "Wish you were here."

But it might not be true for everyone with cameras. Some people might be taking pictures, but might also be seeing Alaska with their own eyes, as well as through the eye of a camera.

So, I guess, it all depends on how you see . . .

One of my favorites statements is from Teilhard de Chardin, "The whole of life can be found in the verb *to see.*"

Photo opportunities can often be missed opportunities for seeing. The camera's eye might see the scene, but is my eye seeing the scene too?

Are you seeing what you're seeing or are you seeing something else?

I do this all the time. I'm usually somewhere else. I'm not in the room. You might be talking, but I'm not listening to you. I'm still listening to a conversation I had with my sister a few days ago.

Are you listening to what you're listening to or are you listening to something else?

Listening . . . seeing . . . being there . . . savoring what's before my eyes. . . or missing everything . . .

It's Saturday afternoon and I'm at my eight-year-old nephew's tenth soccer game of the season. It's still the first half and they're losing by 5 to 1, and I don't even know the score. I'm dying to get back home, to get back to my computer.

Are you watching what you're watching or are you watching something else?

We're at a restaurant. You ordered fish, orange roughy, and I ordered veal parmesan, and I don't taste a bite of what I'm eating. I'm mad because I didn't get a steak and I'm concentrating on a conversation at the next table.

Am I eating what I'm eating or am I eating something else?

I'm munching on potato chips while watching Monday Night Football. I eat every last one and hardly tasted any one of them. My team is losing. Besides that I had a bad day at work. The guy I usually work with called in sick and the boss stuck me with twice the work.

Am I eating what I'm eating or is something eating me?

I guess I'd better turn off the television and take a good look at these snapshots of my life or better still, be in the scenes of my life as they are happening now, today, at this very moment.

The old saying: "Be where you is, because if you be where you ain't, then you ain't where you is," makes good sense.

Not seeing . . . I miss so much.

Last year, driving East on Interstate 80, I enjoyed listening to an audiotape book *Blue Highways: A Journey into America.* The author, William Least-Heat Moon, prefers the blue highways on the maps, the small roads, the roads less traveled. Me: I'm always in a rush. I always prefer an interstate or a two lane highway to smaller roads.

William Least-Heat Moon had some time off from teaching. So he took a slow 13,000-mile, 38-state trip on this country's Blue Highways. As I was traveling sixty-five miles an hour on a red highway, Route 80, he was telling me about all the places he was slowly seeing on this nations wonderful blue highways and byways—places I've never seen or heard about—places like Nameless, Tennessee.

I loved watching all those Charles Kuralt Sunday morning pieces on television introducing us to little known people in little known towns and scenic places I usually miss. One of his comments hit me: "Thanks to the interstate highway system, it is now possible to travel across the country from coast to coast without seeing anything."

Maybe I'd better put my camera down, turn off the tapes, put down my fork, close the bag of potato chips and start watching the soccer game. I'd better start seeing what I'm seeing, eating what I'm eating, hearing what I'm hearing, being "where I'm at!"

Where am I?

Unique

There are over six billion of us on the earth.

Is any one of us truly unique?

Do we do something—at least one thing—that nobody else does?

Well, we all have a different fingerprint.

And our DNA is unique, isn't it?

But is there anything I do that nobody else on the planet does? Is there anything new under the sun? How unique can an individual be?

I don't know. I haven't talked to everyone yet.

Last night as I sat in a small chapel praying, I found myself asking that question: "Is there anything I do that nobody else does?"

Well, I like to make lists, but that's not unique.

Well, I decided to make a list of ten things I do that maybe—just maybe—nobody else does—or ever did. Maybe these ten behaviors are unique.

> 1) When I'm in a cemetery, and when I have time, I always walk around and look at every stone that has a birthday on it to see if there was anyone who died the day I was born.

2) Whenever I go into a church or Jewish synagogue for the first time, I *always* make three prayer wishes, and the first one is always for the people of that place.

3) Whenever I drive by bodies of water, I always make the sign of the cross. If I am alone, I make the sign of the cross in the usual way; when I'm in the car with another person, I just trace a cross on my forehead. For some reason, rivers, lakes and oceans are sacred places to me.

4) Before I get into bed at night, I stand and raise my arms in prayer and say the "Lord's Prayer." Then I determine where the nearest church is, turn toward it and genuflect three times to the Trinity.

5) I like to take written prayers by others and then rewrite them, not with words, but with tiny pictures, putting the whole prayer in my own personal hieroglyphics.

6) I save miniature golf scorecards, especially of games that I win.

7) Years ago, without knowing why, I cut out and saved the face of Tony the Tiger from the front of boxes of Kellogg's Sugar Frosted Flakes. I once had about 250 faces.

8) When I was in the eighth grade, I was caught shooting other kids with my pea shooter in both the Statue of Liberty and Hayden's Planetarium in New York City and was almost thrown out of both.

9) As far as I know I wrote the second shortest poem ever written. The shortest poem is the existential poem, "I / why?" I don't know who wrote it. My poem is almost as short, "You / Who?" and it also rhymes.

10) I have made lists of my ten favorite movies, books, memories, jokes, poems, prayers, Bible texts, interesting people I've met, places I've been, and now ten things that might make me unique.

Memories

I can still picture the scene. My Dad was sitting near the window reading the paper in his favorite chair, a dark green vinyl easy chair with shiny brass tacks.

I was about thirty feet away opening and closing the tiny drawers of our family combination desk and bookcase. I was "moothering"—a Gaelic word for doing—but doing nothing—or for puttering around. I was checking everything inside the desk, opening and closing, picking up, putting down whatever I could find. I must have had nothing else to do. I was eight or nine years old at the time.

Having finished with everything inside the desk, I began opening the books on the shelf that was the upper part of the desk.

In a book of poems that my Father used to read, I found something to bother him with. Something I had never seen before: a dry red rose petal. At first I said, "Ugh" as in ugly, but then a feeling of sacrament came over me. "This must be something sacred." Of course these weren't my conscious thoughts at the time. I didn't know what sacred really meant till I was at least thirty-five; but I sensed that something was sacred here in the way children know sacred.

So I carefully approached my father with the book opened to the page with the red rose petal in it. It was like an offertory procession at church.

"Dad, what's this."

"What's what?" he softly said as he came out from behind his paper.

"This."

He looked at the red rose petal sitting there in the book of poems and he became silent. Then with that smile, which he was so well-known for, he lit up and said just one word, "Memories."

And he gently took the book from me and silently read the poem where the red rose lay and then said, "Thank you."

A memory. A moment with my Dad. A moment from his life.

It was to become one of my favorite memories of my Dad—a scene that I've stored between the pages of my mind—like a red rose petal—and every once in a while, when I haven't much to do, I "moother" with my memories, and there it is, as live as a dry red rose petal.

Memories are snapshots developing in the darkroom of our mind.

The Scream

*H*ave you ever heard someone really scream?

We've all heard cries and seen tears. What I'm talking about here is a scream.

Edvard Munch (1863-1944) is the artist who painted the famous picture, "The Scream." Before it appeared on T-Shirts, coffee mugs, and key chains, it was a "stopper." People don't pause too long to look at paintings, but people stopped to look at Munch's drawing. It hit home. It was home for many people.

People scream. Munch's cartoon like face and figure on a bridge, hands over ears, is screaming. The person is experiencing hell, a bombing, a catastrophic moment.

A scream is a raw sound. It's often loud and long! But sometimes it's an ongoing moan that lasts for days. It's very painful. It's something people don't like to hear or be around.

I once heard one in a long corridor at the Lutheran Hospital in Brooklyn. I was standing outside the operating room with my sister Mary. The rest of our family were downstairs in the lobby waiting.

My Mother was inside the operating room undergoing emergency surgery.

She was the victim of a hit-and-run driver just that morning. She had been on her way to church and to work—aged eighty-four—still very much alive.

The light turned green for her and she began crossing the street. A car came up over the hill, tried to beat the light, hit my Mom—threw her up into the air and she came crashing down onto her head. I'm sure she screamed. She was probably unconscious from that moment on. The car sped away. A crossing guard saw what happened, and heard some screams—perhaps from people on the sidewalk. I don't know.

A priest from the rectory up the street came quickly to anoint my Mom even before the ambulance arrived.

My sister Mary, who lived and worked in that area had been the first to reach the hospital. My sister Peggy was called and rushed in from Long Island. I lived ninety miles away in upstate New York and a friend drove me down immediately. He got me there by eleven o'clock and after tears and hugs in the hospital lobby I learned the doctors were trying everything, operating on her brain, giving her the best of care. But it didn't look good.

Just before noon my sister Mary and I went upstairs to the surgery floor. We were standing in a very long hall, the length of a city block. The surgeon came out and told us that Mom had just died. "We tried every-thing. Sorry."

She asked the surgeon if I could give my mom a last blessing and say a prayer over her. Then we would go down to the lobby and tell the rest of the family the sad news.

Off to the side of this long hospital hallway was a small waiting room. I said to my sister, "Mary, let's go into that room, have a good cry, suck it in, and then go downstairs and tell everyone."

My sister Mary yelled: "Suck it in yourself" and she screamed out, then and there, the loudest scream I've ever heard in my life. It was a "Primal Scream" that came up out of her depths, a scream that echoed and bounced off the walls down, down that long hall. People popped out of every doorway. And then, all was silent. Everyone could see us holding each other—I holding her in her pain, and she holding me in mine.

I've often wondered about my sister's scream. Was it so loud and so primal that it blocked all my tears? It's over ten years now and I still haven't cried over mother's death.

I cried when my nephew, Michael, died suddenly of cancer at fifteen.

I cried when my dad died of cancer at sixty-seven.

And I cried when my brother, Billy, died of cancer at fifty-one.

I've wondered till this day, "Was my sister's scream so loud, so heart-breaking, that she screamed for both of us?"

I don't know.

Or do I have a scream, a "primal scream" that is yet to come?

Hat

He was wearing a hat in the house and it made him look stupid.

Fortunately, I didn't say anything.

Inside the recording studio of my brain, I was saying, "Wearing a hat in the house makes you look odd!"

Then I remembered my brother and his hat. Four of us, my brother, his wife, my mom and I drove to Baltimore for lunch at Tio Pepe's restaurant. We walked in and were brought to a table. Just after we sat down, a waiter walked over to my brother and sort of quietly said, "Sir, you'll have to take off your hat."

There was a moment of hesitation on my brother's part. I started to feel a rush of anger move up through my chest towards my lips. I was about to say, "Please! Let him wear his hat." My brother was quicker than I. He always was. He smiled to the waiter, said a soft "Okay," and took off his hat.

Thank God he was funny that day. It stopped all of us from thinking about his head. He had lost most of his hair. His head was bloated. It had lots of nicks and cuts—as if he had gotten a hair cut from a blind barber.

The meal was great. Mysteriously that month, my brother's taste buds had come back. Chemotherapy and cancer—melanoma and a brain tumor—can do a number on someone. While eating from his own plate, he kept stealing food from Mom, his wife, Joanne, and me. He wanted to taste everything at one of Baltimore's finest restaurants.

It was the last meal I had with him. I drove back to New York that afternoon. A month later he was dead.

I remember resolving in that restaurant that I would never ask anyone to take off their hat.

I had forgotten.

Here I was wanting someone to take off their hat in the house. Realizing what I was thinking, I smiled. My motivation and my intention were still the same. As with my brother, I didn't want him to look stupid. Thank God for memories.

Economics 101

*N*obody ever really wanted to take Economics 101 at Upper Glendale Community College. Those who did, took it because it was a sure B or C because of a history of easy professors or simply because they needed another course and Economics 101 fitted well into their schedule.

That is till Professor Nancy Money applied and was accepted to teach the course at UGCC. She was fresh out of graduate school and hadn't finished her Ph.D. yet. This was a chance for her to make some money, pay her bills, and begin her teaching career.

Those sixteen freshmen were certainly surprised when Professor Money asked them to put their money on their desks. "I'd like to begin this first class in Economics by asking everyone to put all the money you have with you on your desk and count it. This is not a hold-up and this is not a collection!"

Some students were amused. Some were confused. Some were semi-awake, but people began reaching into their wallets or the pockets of their jeans and put their money on their desks.

"Now, will each of you tell me how much money you're carrying?"

"$11.63 and two credit cards," came the first response from Jill, a student in center seat first row.

"Wait a minute!" Professor Money said. "All I want to know is how much *cash* each of your has on your person this morning."

"$5.75."

"19.34."

"27.16."

"$16.54."

"Seventy-five cents."

That got a laugh.

"Two cents."

That also got a laugh.

"Just kidding. $33.22."

"$95.00."

That got a "Wow!" and some twists of the head to see who belonged to the voice.

"$17.89—but I also have a folded $20 bill for an emergency that I have had hidden here in my wallet since I was thirteen years old. I've never taken it out. And I'm leaving it in there for good luck. It's worked so far. I've never been without money since I put it there."

"$15.00," the answers continued.

"$5.15."

"$11.25."

"$9.00."

"$1.00 but I do have about $15.00 in coins in my car."

"$16.00."

"$4.75."

"Thank you! Any comments?"

There were no comments. There was just wonder about what all this was getting at.

"Now how many of you have credit cards with you?"

Everyone raised their hands.

"Thank you," Professor Money said. "Now since Economics is about cash and credit, about buying and selling, basically about money, I would like each of you now to estimate or to use the new word on the market, 'guesstimate'—how much money this first year of college is going to cost you. Include clothing, transportation, food, books, tuition, etc. List everything you can think of. Any questions?"

Jason Gridwell, a short freckle faced kid, asked, "Is that really your real name?"

"You mean, 'Nancy'?"

"No, a, I mean 'Money'."

"Yes! I come from the Money tree."

That got a good laugh.

In fact, kids stopped slouching and semi-sleeping and began sitting up after that. The atmosphere in the room changed then and would never be the same again.

"Wow!" People said to themselves. "Maybe we do have a class here after all. This looks like it's going to be good. Cool. Money is interesting."

"Jason," Professor Money asked, "why did you ask?"

"Well, I was wondering, did you choose to become an economist because of your name?"

Probably, several in the class, and I suppose many who went through the UGCC catalogue, wondered the same thing.

"No, but I've been asked that question a thousand times before in college and graduate school. People have told me about all kinds of names that match professions. There's a Dr. Hertz in Pennsylvania who is a dentist.

There's a proctologist named Dr. Bottoms. There are firefighters with the name of Burns. There's a psychologist, I think in New York, named Dr. Looney and a cardiologist in Boston named Dr. Hart. There's a pediatrician in Georgia named Dr. Childs. There's a florist in Indiana named Flowers and a podiatrist in Florida named Dr. Foote."

The class of sixteen students were really listening to that litany of names giving it their full attention and lots of smiles.

Dr. Nancy Money was quick, bright, perky and very much alive.

What happened next totally surprised everyone.

From behind her desk she took a big blue shopping bag. "I have here four Monopoly games. There are sixteen of you, so I'm going to have you break into four groups of four. I'd like you to play Monopoly for forty-five minutes. As you know the game Monopoly can go on forever, and we only have sixteen classes this semester, so I changed the rules of the game somewhat to speed it up for this class. When you open the box you'll notice that there are four white envelopes in each box. Each of you is to take one envelope. Inside the envelope there will be instructions, money and cards that tell what property you already own, houses and hotels you might already have on those properties. They will be in the envelopes. If you have any questions, just ask. The oldest throws the dice first to get going—and then go clockwise. Thank you.

Excitement, smiles, puzzlement, filled the room as the students moved their desks together in fours and opened up their Monopoly box. As indicated, each box had four white envelopes.

On opening her envelope, a student named Jane discovered she already owned hotels on Boardwalk and Park Place, as well as Pennsylvania, Pacific and North Carolina. She owned that whole side of the board, the blue and the green spots. Not only that, she had $60,000 in cash in her envelope.

Penny opened her envelope to discover she had no money or property in her envelope, and she was in jail.

Each person began the game on different terms, with different amounts of money. They had never seen or played Monopoly like this before. Some people were out of the game in three rolls of the dice.

After about forty minutes of Monopoly, Professor Money said, "Game's over! Put everything back in the Monopoly boxes." They did. "Now just stand and walk around or stand anywhere and chat with another person, just one person, about what you were thinking and feeling during the game."

They did. It was quite lively. People were talking to strangers. People were getting to know one another.

Then Professor Money asked everyone to put their desks back into their regular places. "We have about twenty minutes class time left. Any comments?"

There were!

Kids talked about fairness and unfairness. There were the usual clichés about the rich getting richer and the poor getting poorer. People said that they never thought of the game Monopoly as connected to real life. They never thought of people starting off in life as "Big shots! Little shots! And some people who have no real shot at life at all." Missy, who had already made it as a cheerleader at UGCC, said, "I don't think life is like rolling dice." Others vehemently disagreed with her.

The bell rang.

Economics 101 was on its way.

Kids couldn't wait to tell friends about their experience. "I picked a winner!"

And winner it was.

Before the end of that first semester those sixteen students visited a bank, had a tour of the vaults, the Manager's office, computer rooms, etc.

Before the end of that first semester, thanks to a suggestion from Professor Money, those sixteen students had pooled their money, formed a small corporation and invested in ten stocks which they choose, but they had to have three stocks that were in companies outside the United States.

Before the end of that first semester those sixteen students had visited the State Capital and met with State Representatives, seven of whom were freshmen themselves, about local, state and federal budgets.

Before the end of that first semester those sixteen students divided into teams of four and interviewed store managers in the local mall to compare their business and budgets with those of similar downtown stores.

Before the end of that first semester those sixteen students also interviewed the managers of two local movie theaters and the managers of two video stores to compare their budgets.

Economics 101 certainly taught everyone about how little they knew about zoning laws, where tax money goes, the issue of medical benefits, the cost of road repairs, city, county, state and federal politics.

Dr. Nancy Money was a demanding professor. She got students thinking, questioning, reading, and seeing many implications they never saw before as well as how so much on this earth is intertwined.

After that first semester, everyone wanted to take Economics 101 at Upper Glendale Community College.

Professor Nancy Money? She did finish her Ph. D. while teaching that first year at UGCC. The second year, she married Larry Diamond. (No, he's not a jeweler. But he is a mining engineer.)

Apples and Oranges

Sometimes we see the forest and we miss the trees.

Sometimes we talk about apples and oranges and never really taste one.

"Take and eat!"

I once heard a speaker tell a story about Jean Piaget. Piaget is the French psychologist, who was a major specialist on how little children at different stages of their development think and see very differently from adults. This story about Piaget caught my attention. I was somewhere else. Who listens to most of the stuff that is spoken at them in talks anyway? If we hear anything, it's usually the specific, an example, a personal story in the middle of a whole flock of words flying over our heads.

Piaget had the honesty and humility to tell this story about himself. For me, it was one of those "Life's Teaching Moments." The best ones are usually those we learn about ourselves from ourselves—usually after a dumb fall. But we sometimes learn from the lives of others. I was getting the story second- or third- hand from the speaker, but I got it. And I think I got it because it was very specific.

The story went something like this: Once upon a time, Jean Piaget was walking with his young son on a Fall afternoon. Suddenly they heard the sound of geese flying overhead. The boy stopped. The honking sounds had captured his entire attention. He was at an age when everything was new and exciting. He had never heard the sound of geese before. Surprised, speechless, looking up, he began pointing to the geese flying way above them. His mouth was gasping in excitement. His father pointed to them and without any emotion said, "Geese. They are geese." The boy stopped looking. A short time later the same thing happened again. This time the boy raised his head but quickly lowered it and kept walking. Sensing what had happened, Piaget became emotional with an adult's feeling of guilt. He had ruined the *specific*—the special moment—with the *abstract*. He had labeled this mighty surge of energy, this rush of life flying above them as merely "geese," and his son might never see geese again as he saw them that first time.

Unless we see with the eyes of a child, we won't see the kingdom of heaven around us.

It's like the difference between a veteran season ticket-holder entering the stadium, and a kid coming up the ramp and seeing the great green major league baseball field for the first time: the wonder, the awe.

Seeing something for the hundredth time is very different from seeing it the first time.

Numbers can numb us . . .

Numbers can throw us . . .

Mother Teresa said that she didn't see numbers. "I see individuals."

How did the Sisters of St. Joseph ever teach us at O.L.P.H. grammar school in Brooklyn, N.Y. in the early fifties? We must have had close to a hundred kids in every class.

Our vision is blurred by the "so much" and the "so many."

Someone unwraps a box of chocolates, lifts the cover, shows us the chocolates and we don't know which one to take.

Once a former student wrote to me, "The trees are now a blur. I don't see trees like I used to see them." He had moved from the countryside in Wisconsin to the city of Chicago. He had joined the rat race.

We move too fast. We miss the forest and we miss the trees.

When we eat an apple or an orange slowly, when we savor its juices, we're being very "specific."

Life is the specific. The joy of life is fascination with the specific: this dog named "Polly," this cat named "Bufford," this trophy I received for winning the spelling bee in the sixth grade, this dresser that was my Aunt Harriet's, this person I'm married to, this friend I drive to work each day.

The Vietnamese Buddhist monk, Thich Nhat Hanh, goes around the world preaching *mindfulness*. Slow down. Be mindful. Taste the day. Taste the apple. Feel the hug. Look the other in the eye. Be mindful of each step. Pay attention.

It's a variation of the old saying, "Don't hurry, don't worry, and smell the flowers along the way."

The U.S. Post Office once published a stamp replicating Georgia O'Keeffe's painting, "Red Poppy, 1927." If you bought a sheet of these stamps, it included a picture of Georgia O'Keeffe and her words, "Nobody sees a flower, really—it is so small—we haven't time, and to see takes time, like to have a friend takes time."

Someone said, "You can have twenty years' experience or one year's experience twenty times.

T. S. Eliot wrote, "We had the experience but missed the meaning."

Mindfulness takes time. Enjoying an apple or an orange takes time. Stopping to be fascinated by geese flying south for the winter takes time.

Dominoes, Boomerangs, and Butterflies

I've heard of the "The Domino Effect," "The Boomerang Effect," but I had never heard about "The Butterfly Effect."

In fact, when I heard it, I blurted out, "Are they kidding?"

They aren't. The theory goes something like this: "The butterfly that shakes its wings in China this week affects the weather in America next week."

That's hard to believe. Yet, where and why does the wind start? Why does it stop? There are millions and millions of birds and bugs shaking their wings all over the world, so why aren't we having more hurricanes?

"We're not," I suppose those who propose the theory would say, "precisely because of 'The Butterfly Effect.'"

Everything affects everything.

Everything has consequences.

Now there's a bumper sticker slogan. Or a fortune cookie fortune. A message we'd better keep posted in the office of our mind or on our bathroom mirror, so we can see it as we start each day.

"You realize, there are consequences."

That's advice we tend to block out at times. We want to wish it away, but if we do, we become "wishy washy."

Everything we do has consequences.

Our past catches up with us.

The boomerang comes flying back towards the person who throws it.

Use a land mine and someday, someone you least expect, might step it. Boom!

Promiscuous sex affects your life the next day, the next night, the rest of your life.

"You're kidding!"

"I'm not. There has to be a morning after . . . "

People contract AIDS. A kid can become pregnant. People feel guilt. They come to lose the depths of the meaning of themselves, of their worth, of their behavior, of their sexuality and what relationships and commit-ment mean.

Each commitment affects every commitment.

Everything has consequences.

Each lie makes the next lie easier—weakening the fabric of our being, weakening the power of our words, weakening our perceptions of the value of ourselves and others. We stop looking into the eyes of the person we lied to—and to the next person, and the next person, and to the person after that, and on and on and on . . .

It's hard to look at ourselves in the bathroom mirror after we flushed some of the truth down the toilet.

Original sins and unoriginal sins sink down into the origins of our being.

Thank God, it also works the other way.

Love begets love; truth begets truth; service begets service.

Each time we are honest, each time we reach out in love to help our family, our neighbor, the stranger, each time we compliment another, it's a butterfly that flies around the world, a rock skipping across the water, a stone tossed into a pond where the circles keep expanding, a boomerang that brings that honesty and love back to us.

I love the adage, "So live that you can sell your parrot to the town gossip and have nothing to fear."

Gossip begets gossip.

Fear begets fear.

Love begets love.

Life is a chess game. Each move we make has implications for the next move on the board.

Like dominos falling, every action has a reaction.

We often stress freedom of choice and individuality and "doing one's own thing," without bringing up the question of consequences.

There are covenants in all of creation. Tear them and we begin to rip ourselves apart along with all of creation around us.

Butterflies and bugs, birds and flowers, trees and air, oceans and what lives in them, better not get messed up.

Some people poo-poo environmentalists!

In 1997 coral researchers began discovering that more and more coral reefs around the world are rapidly dying because of disease—some of which scientists don't know enough about. Answers are speculative, but the dumping of sewage and other waste materials are in police line-up as possible culprits.

Awareness of the inevitability of consequences can lead individuals, groups, and nations to go the other way. We can and must work to stop pollution and clean the air and the oceans, protect fish and birds, and the millions of tiny species of life that we can't see, but now know are affected by our behavior.

All this is not new. As kids we heard the verse, "A little neglect may breed great mischief . . . for want of a nail the shoe was lost; for want of a shoe the horse was lost; and for want of a horse the rider was lost."

And the proverbs:

"A stitch in time saves nine."

"What goes around comes around."

"Those who live by the sword, die by the sword."

Be aware of *The Domino Effect*.

Be aware of *The Boomerang Effect*.

Be aware of *The Butterfly Effect!*

There are consequences.

I'm Repeating Myself

At what age does a person say, "I'm repeating myself?"

How old do we have to be to discover that we're doing the same thing over and over again—all our lives?

We are creatures of habit. We are our virtues and our vices, our strengths and weaknesses. Deja vu is a good description for so much of what we do.

Sandra got "involved" with four men in a row. All four were described as "losers" by her family and friends. "Be careful," they said, "he seems to be a repeat performance of that last guy you were dating." She wouldn't listen, that is, till she *really* got burnt. Then she said, "It's not *them*. It's *I*. I'm the loser for always picking losers." So she stepped back, stopped dating for a year, and looked before she leaped. Then she met a wonderful man, dated him for quite a while, and then married. Everything is working out fine.

Have you ever been driving in the left lane of a two lane highway and the car just ahead of you, but in the right lane, suddenly starts to move into your lane without warning, without signals, without looking. We brake. We beep. We scream. They swerve quickly back into the right lane and a crash is avoided. Then you see a big dent in their left side, right where you would have hit them.

History repeats itself.

It's easier to see this in others than to see it in ourselves. But when we do, when we see that we are repeat offenders, it can be a grace.

Aged thirty-five, I'm playing a game of half-court basketball—two against two. I'm out there on the perimeter dribbling the ball not sure whether to drive or pass. I begin noticing that the guy who is covering me is not standing directly in front of me. He's off to my right. Still dribbling I say, "How come you're covering me *funny?*" He says, "I noticed that you can't drive to your left, so why should I stand directly in front of you." I passed the ball.

After thousands of basketball games in high school and college, I didn't know that about myself.

What else am I doing that I don't even know that I'm doing? What are my patterns?

Once in high school, I was "stuck" for a paper for English class. I was probably spending too much time playing basketball or being lazy. I don't remember that part of the story. What to do? Time was closing in. I remembered an essay that I had written the year before that I thought was good. The teacher didn't. It came back with two short words in red and a mark on the last page. "Very poor. 74." Luckily, I had saved it. I found loose leaf paper that matched perfectly as well as a ball point pen that had the same color blue ink. Carefully I took out the staple on the top of the pages of the old essay. Then I rewrote that last page and carefully stapled it together. I handed my paper in for a re-run. Three days later my essay came back covered in red. There were comments and suggestions everywhere. I quickly turned to the last page. I wanted to know the bottom line: "Very good, 94."

Both teachers are now dead. Both these teachers were so different. The first teacher had a lot more outside interests than being in a classroom. He often said he hated marking papers. The second teacher was tough. I didn't get too many 94's from him, but he was very interested in teaching us how to write. Essays and stories came back covered in red—covered with comments like: "Too many adjectives here." "Try shorter sentences.

Remember Hemingway." "You have three paragraphs here in this one paragraph."

Back then I had figured out some of the patterns of both these teachers, but I didn't know my own. I now realize that I'm still doing what I did back then—passing off old stuff, old stories, old patterns, as new, sometimes out of laziness, but sometimes discovering what some thought was "poor" others might think enriching.

I'm repeating myself.

What does it take to discover this: a family intervention, a crash, a question, a deadline? Maybe then we can write the new story, meet new people, move another way, and look before we move to the left.

Judgment Days

*B*efore we get to them, most days look the same on the calendar. Every day is just a day, a number, that is, till we get out of bed that morning. Then the differences begin.

Some days are judgment days. We don't plan them, but they're there. We have a lump, so we make an appointment with the doctor. Today is the day. Or today is the day for a job review. Or we're relaxing after supper, reading the paper, and we see the obituary notice of someone we know, someone our own age, who has died suddenly. Without planning on it, it's at that moment we begin to think about our whole life.

Judgment days. Albert Camus once wrote, "I shall tell you a great secret, my friend. Do not wait for the last judgment. It takes place every day."

One of those days on the calendar is our death day—hopefully not this year, but some year, some day.

"After death comes the judgment . . . "

After we die, at the wake, our family, friends, acquaintances, will make judgments about us . . . who we were . . . what we were like . . . how we were connected . . . what we meant to them . . . stories, memories, moments we shared . . .

The official and unofficial eulogies will be attempts to sum us up . . . judgments about us and our time on this earth.

The obituary in the newspaper will give just the bare bones of our life: date of birth, date of death, family members, and sometimes places of work, accomplishments and groups we belonged to.

Almost all of these judgments at the time of our death will be positive. We praise our dead.

The short summaries people make at someone's death are often accurate judgments—containing truth about the person. When we listen to what is said and not said, we get glimpses of who a person was. Not everyone gets the following accolades:

> "Honest."
>
> "Hard worker."
>
> "Friend."
>
> "Never said a bad word about anyone."
>
> "Someone you could always count on.
>
> "A good sense of humor."
>
> "A good dad."
>
> "A great mom . . . so understanding."
>
> "A person of faith."
>
> "Always there when you needed him."
>
> "A joy to be with."

But before we die, there are other judgment days.

When we ourselves step back and take a good look at our life, we see those days, those moments, that were particular judgment days. Often they're the ones that were negative and quite painful.

We were deeply in love, had no doubts about marrying this special person, and he or she suddenly ends the relationship. It's a shock to the system. We're devastated, wiped out. We become quiet. We begin to judge ourselves as worthless. We're a nothing. We feel empty and stupid.

Divorces often do the same thing, not just to those going through one, but also to kids, at times.

Or we don't get the job, even though there were three interviews, even though we were complimented for having such a good resume.

Or we're "fired" or "terminated" or leave a job and nobody pronounces a word of praise or "thanks" for our years of service.

Judgment days can be terrifying days in our life; they can also be marvelous moments of reconsideration and rejoicing.

Couples celebrating their Twenty-fifth or Fiftieth Wedding Anniversary sit there at the head table hearing their children praising them, pointing clear particulars that meant so much to them. Moments like that are judgment moments that make it all so worth it.

Or a friend tells us about their marriage, how empty it is, how "He's married to the TV or the computer. It's his mistress." And we pause and reflect upon our marriage and in comparison we are quite grateful.

Poems, plays, songs, novels and movies bring many a person to judgment moments. Here are two poems, the first by William Shakespeare and the second by John Crowe Ransom that can trigger serious reflection.

Sonnet II

When forty winters shall besiege thy brow,
And dig deep trenches in they beauty's field,
Thy youth's proud livery, so gazed on now,
Will be a tatter'd weed, of small worth held:
Then being ask'd where all thy beauty lies,
Where all the treasure of thy lusty days,
To say, within thine own deep-sunken eyes,
Were an all-eating shame and thriftless praise.
How much more praise deserved thy beauty's use,
If thou couldst answer 'This child of mine
Shall sum my count and make my old excuse,'
Proving his beauty by succession thine!
This were to be new made when thou art old,
And see thy blood warm when thou feel'st it cold.

Blue Girls

Twirling your blue skirts, travelling the sward
Under the towers of your seminary,
Go listen to your teachers old and contrary
Without believing a word.
Tie the white fillets then about your lustrous hair
And think no more of what will come to pass
Than bluebirds that go walking on the grass
And chattering on the air.
Practice your beauty, blue girls, before it fail;
And I will cry with my loud lips and publish
Beauty which all our power shall never establish,
It is so frail.
For I could tell you a story that is true:
I know a lady with a terrible tongue,
Blear eyes fallen from blue,
All her perfections tarnished—and yet it is not long
Since she was lovelier than any of you.

Erik Erikson doesn't give an exact age for his eighth and last stage of life. He calls it "Integrity vs. Despair." It's the stage when a person realizes he or she is running out of time, so they read and carefully re-read the story of their life.

Hopefully, we are comfortable with our life. We accept the reality. We have made mistakes. We see our accomplishments. We feel a sense of integrity or wholeness and we are not afraid to die.

Others despair. They see too many mistakes, too many loose ends, that have unraveled their life. The garment of self has too many holes and rips in it. We have failed.

Christ often talks about judgment. "Make an account of your stewardship." He also teaches its not too late to enter the garden. It's never too late to cry out for forgiveness. The Good Thief stole heaven in the last minute of his life.

A Person of Substance

"*N*o substance!"

Hearing that criticism is the fear of every writer, teacher, preacher, every human being. I once heard a preacher described as, "All fluff, no stuff."

Who wants to be thought of as shallow or phony or a Pharisee?

No one wants to be described as "running on empty."

"It's the sizzle that sells the steak," but at some point, if your steaks are too tough or too fatty, or not cooked properly, people will go to another restaurant.

Your smile is great; the story behind your scar is sad; but at some point, the issue is beneath "skin deep."

Jean Kerr, in her book, *The Snake Has All the Lines,* wrote, "I'm tired of all this business about beauty being only skin-deep. That's deep enough. What do you want—an adorable pancreas?"

Now, of course, we hope those we love have a healthy pancreas. However, we know there's much more to a person.

Much more.

And the more refers to issues of substance.

We want our most important relationships to go from our center to the other's center, to go beneath the skin, to the heart, to the pulse of each other—in short, to have substance—to be a person of substance.

After the honeymoon, after the mirror clears from its steam, we learn that beauty is more than skin and figure, youth and bend.

As Stephen Leacock put it, "Many a man in love with a dimple makes the mistake of marrying the whole girl."

Of course, there are similar sayings for women—referring to falling in love with his looks, his eyes, his laugh, his job, his wallet or his car.

Dr. Laura Schlessinger gives equal billing to men and women when they act stupidly. Check out her two books: *Ten Stupid Things Women Do to Mess up Their Lives* and *Ten Stupid Things Men Do to Mess up Their Lives*.

Obviously beauty helps. It's a great starter.

But, beauty, both external and internal, is relatively subjective.

When surprised about "opposites" being attracted to each other, we've all said, "Beauty lies in the eye of the beholder." Isn't that one of the great realities of life? We all see each other differently. Some call it chemistry; some call it mystery. I see this other person as beautiful according to my own way of seeing. I want to spend time with this person—and sometimes that means a lifetime. Beauty is a great golden cord that binds relationships together—but it's subjective beauty.

Or sometimes what keeps us together is fear; sometimes it's children; or pride: the inability to admit I've made a mistake; or commitment: I made a vow, I gave my word; and sometimes it's an ongoing illusion.

But for a relationship to be truly lasting, truly authentic, there must be *substance*.

What does it mean to be a "person of substance?"

To me a person of substance—down-deep substance—is someone who has integrity, honesty, humility, humor, strength, significance, presence, grace, power, maturity, stick-to-itiveness, and reliability. A tall order finding one!

It's the call of every person—to be a person of substance—to move toward being in the image and likeness of God.

One of the most popular definitions of God from the Middle Ages comes from St. John of Damascus. "God is a sea of infinite substance." I like that.

"God is a sea of infinite substance."

And I am made in the image and likeness of God.

I am called to walk this earth as a person of substance.

In the story of The Prodigal Son, there is a devastating description of the younger brother after he has left home: "And not many days after, the younger son gathered all together, and took his journey into a far country, and there he wasted his substance with riotous living."

A person can waste his substance . . . Have I?

The Ceiling Fan Keeps Spinning

The Earth will keep spinning long after we've died and been buried in the earth.

The ceiling fan keeps spinning after we've shut it off.

Watch. Listen. Learn.

Ceitling fans can create an atmosphere for thinking. Air conditioners don't do it—at least for me.

I suppose the questions are: During my time on Earth, what am I doing to make this Earth the Garden Paradise that God wills it to be? Am I planting trees for future generations or am I eating forbidden fruit? Am I hiding from God in the bushes or am I working with God as partner in the heat of the day and then walking with God in the cool of the evening? Am I being a servant to my brothers and sisters? Am I concerned only with the here or only with the hereafter or both?

The Earth is listening carefully for our responses to these questions. It has a vested interest in our answers.

If we perceive Earth to be a Garden Paradise, a home that we are going to will to others, then we'll take good care of it. Rented cars or apartments often don't get the careful treatment people give to their own car or house.

From the experiences of life: riding our first bike, working a garden, going to a Chinese restaurant or going out for ice cream, buying a Christmas present, seeing a play, being hit with a death in the family, listening and watching each other, especially our family, we can learn life's lessons.

From Adam and Eve we can learn the lesson that God has given us basic choices. We need to make and keep the covenant with creation. When we don't, Earth stops being Paradise. We need to sit under a tree with God and each other and reflect upon all this. We need to learn knowledge of good and evil and then put goodness into practice.

From Moses we can learn that people enslave people forcing them to do cheap labor. Moreover, we might notice that enslaved people sometimes prefer chains to freedom, the known to the unknown. Calling people out of slavery is a difficult exodus. People need a dream, a Promised Land, a vision of something better. Then it takes strong personalities, miracles, willingness to break addictions, and then many years of perseverance to bring about the dream, to have a land of milk and honey.

From Isaiah and the Old Testament prophets we can learn that we have eyes to see, ears to hear, but we don't always use them. Often we don't see the poor, the blind and the lame, right in our midst. Often we don't struggle to come home from our exiles.

From the Buddha we can learn that desire can be a fire that can burn us. Consumerism can consume us. Stuff can make us feel stuffed.

From Aristotle we can learn the importance of asking questions, doing research, checking things out, observing, classifying, making distinctions, trying to understand "the stuff" of earth.

From Jesus, the New Adam, we can learn the importance of sitting under the tree of the cross. We can learn that the cross is not only the tree of the knowledge of good and evil, but it's also the tree of life. Sitting under the cross we see people cursing, spitting and killing one another. We can also see Jesus responding with love and forgiveness. We need to keep reflecting on Jesus' words, "Greater love than this no one has, that they lay down their life for their friends," as well as, "Father forgive them, for they don't know what they are doing."

We can discover that Jesus is someone who was very much of the Earth:

~ a carpenter who knew wood and what it takes to build a strong home;

~ a mystic who learned lessons from the flowers of the field, the birds of the air, fig trees and how farmers sow seeds;

~ a teacher who loved to mingle in marketplaces, listen to tales about fathers and sons, and how people shun those with leprosy;

~ a true Israelite who went to the temple to pray, but first noticed poor widows putting in their two cents, so unlike those caught up in show, or law, or place, wanting to appear more important than others;

~ a God-searcher who often escaped into the wilderness to listen for God's will;

~ a brother who calls us to follow him as the Way, the Truth and the Life;

~ a person who walked our Earth, challenged people to enter into a kingdom of love, was rejected, crucified, died and was buried, and then rose again on the third day, the New Earth, the New Creation, the Lord of History, the Lord of All Story.

Jesus grew in wisdom, age and grace. He was down to earth, but he kept looking up.

By being down to earth, but looking up, we too can grow in wisdom, age and grace.

The ceiling fan keeps spinning after we shut it off.

The Earth will keep spinning long after we've died and been buried in the Earth.

But we keep looking up, believing in a New Heavens and a New Earth, with Jesus, the Lord of History, the Lord of All Story.